Diversity of Life

elevate science

MODULES

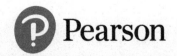

Pearson

Boston, Massachusetts   Chandler, Arizona
Glenview, Illinois   New York, New York

AUTHORS

You're an author!

As you write in this science book, your answers and personal discoveries will be recorded for you to keep, making this book unique to you. That is why you are one of the primary authors of this book.

✏ **In the space below, print your name, school, town, and state. Then write a short autobiography that includes your interests and accomplishments.**

YOUR NAME ....

SCHOOL ....

TOWN, STATE ....

AUTOBIOGRAPHY ....

....

....

....

....

....

Your Photo

Pearson Education, Inc. 330 Hudson Street, New York, NY 10013

Next Generation Science Standards is a registered trademark of Achieve. Neither Achieve nor the lead states and partners that developed the Next Generation Science Standards were involved in the production of this product, and do not endorse it. NGSS Lead States. 2013. *Next Generation Science Standards: For States, By States.* Washington, DC: The National Academies Press.

The cover photo shows a Spanish Shawl nudibranch.

Front cover: Spanish Shawl, NatalieJean/Shutterstock; Back cover: Science Doodle, LHF Graphics/Shutterstock.

ISBN-13: 978-1-418-29158-7
ISBN-10:   1-418-29158-7
4   19

Program Authors

ZIPPORAH MILLER, Ed.D.
Coordinator for K-12 Science Programs, Anne Arundel County Public Schools
Dr. Zipporah Miller currently serves as the Senior Manager for Organizational Learning with the Anne Arundel County Public School System. Prior to that she served as the K-12 Coordinator for science in Anne Arundel County. She conducts national training to science stakeholders on the Next Generation Science Standards. Dr. Miller also served as the Associate Executive Director for Professional Development Programs and conferences at the National Science Teachers Association (NSTA) and served as a reviewer during the development of Next Generation Science Standards. Dr. Miller holds a doctoral degree from the University of Maryland College Park, a master's degree in school administration and supervision from Bowie State University and a bachelor's degree from Chadron State College.

MICHAEL J. PADILLA, Ph.D.
Professor Emeritus, Eugene P. Moore School of Education, Clemson University, Clemson, South Carolina
Michael J. Padilla taught science in middle and secondary schools, has more than 30 years of experience educating middle-school science teachers, and served as one of the writers of the 1996 U.S. National Science Education Standards. In recent years Mike has focused on teaching science to English Language Learners. His extensive experience as Principal Investigator on numerous National Science Foundation and U.S. Department of Education grants resulted in more than $35 million in funding to improve science education. He served as president of the National Science Teachers Association, the world's largest science teaching organization, in 2005–6.

MICHAEL E. WYSESSION, Ph.D
Professor of Earth and Planetary Sciences, Washington University, St. Louis, Missouri
Author of more than 100 science and science education publications, Dr. Wysession was awarded the prestigious National Science Foundation Presidential Faculty Fellowship and Packard Foundation Fellowship for his research in geophysics, primarily focused on using seismic tomography to determine the forces driving plate tectonics. Dr. Wysession is also a leader in geoscience literacy and education; he is the chair of the Earth Science Literacy Initiative, the author of several popular video lectures on geology in the *Great Courses* series, and a lead writer of the *Next Generation Science Standards**.

REVIEWERS

Program Consultants

Carol Baker
Science Curriculum

Dr. Carol K. Baker is superintendent for Lyons Elementary K-8 School District in Lyons, Illinois. Prior to this, she was Director of Curriculum for Science and Music in Oak Lawn, Illinois. Before this she taught Physics and Earth Science for 18 years. In the recent past, Dr. Baker also wrote assessment questions for ACT (EXPLORE and PLAN), was elected president of the Illinois Science Teachers Association from 2011–2013, and served as a member of the Museum of Science and Industry (Chicago) advisory board. She is a writer of the Next Generation Science Standards. Dr. Baker received her B.S. in Physics and a science teaching certification. She completed her master's of Educational Administration (K-12) and earned her doctorate in Educational Leadership.

Jim Cummins
ELL

Dr. Cummins's research focuses on literacy development in multilingual schools and the role technology plays in learning across the curriculum. *Elevate Science* incorporates research-based principles for integrating language with the teaching of academic content based on Dr. Cummins's work.

Elfrieda Hiebert
Literacy

Dr. Hiebert, a former primary-school teacher, is President and CEO of TextProject, a non-profit aimed at providing open-access resources for instruction of beginning and struggling readers, She is also a research associate at the University of California Santa Cruz. Her research addresses how fluency, vocabulary, and knowledge can be fostered through appropriate texts, and her contributions have been recognized through awards such as the Oscar Causey Award for Outstanding Contributions to Reading Research (Literacy Research Association, 2015), Research to Practice award (American Educational Research Association, 2013), and the William S. Gray Citation of Merit Award for Outstanding Contributions to Reading Research (International Reading Association, 2008).

Content Reviewers

Alex Blom, Ph.D.
Associate Professor
Department Of Physical Sciences
Alverno College
Milwaukee, Wisconsin

Joy Branlund, Ph.D.
Department of Physical Science
Southwestern Illinois College
Granite City, Illinois

Judy Calhoun
Associate Professor
Physical Sciences
Alverno College
Milwaukee, Wisconsin

Stefan Debbert
Associate Professor of Chemistry
Lawrence University
Appleton, Wisconsin

Diane Doser
Professor
Department of Geological Sciences
University of Texas at El Paso
El Paso, Texas

Rick Duhrkopf, Ph.D.
Department of Biology
Baylor University
Waco, Texas

Jennifer Liang
University of Minnesota Duluth
Duluth, Minnesota

Heather Mernitz, Ph.D.
Associate Professor of Physical Sciences
Alverno College
Milwaukee, Wisconsin

Joseph McCullough, Ph.D.
Cabrillo College
Aptos, California

Katie M. Nemeth, Ph.D.
Assistant Professor
College of Science and Engineering
University of Minnesota Duluth
Duluth, Minnesota

Maik Pertermann
Department of Geology
Western Wyoming Community College
Rock Springs, Wyoming

Scott Rochette
Department of the Earth Sciences
The College at Brockport
 State University of New York
Brockport, New York

David Schuster
Washington University in St Louis
St. Louis, Missouri

Shannon Stevenson
Department of Biology
University of Minnesota Duluth
Duluth, Minnesota

Paul Stoddard, Ph.D.
Department of Geology and
 Environmental Geosciences
Northern Illinois University
DeKalb, Illinois

Nancy Taylor
American Public University
Charles Town, West Virginia

Teacher Reviewers

Jennifer Bennett, M.A.
Memorial Middle School
Tampa, Florida

Sonia Blackstone
Lake County Schools
Howey In the Hills, Florida

Teresa Bode
Roosevelt Elementary
Tampa, Florida

Tyler C. Britt, Ed.S.
Curriculum & Instructional
 Practice Coordinator
Raytown Quality Schools
Raytown, Missouri

A. Colleen Campos
Grandview High School
Aurora, Colorado

Ronald Davis
Riverview Elementary
Riverview, Florida

Coleen Doulk
Challenger School
Spring Hill, Florida

Mary D. Dube
Burnett Middle School
Seffner, Florida

Sandra Galpin
Adams Middle School
Tampa, Florida

Margaret Henry
Lebanon Junior High School
Lebanon, Ohio

Christina Hill
Beth Shields Middle School
Ruskin, Florida

Judy Johnis
Gorden Burnett Middle School
Seffner, Florida

Karen Y. Johnson
Beth Shields Middle School
Ruskin, Florida

Jane Kemp
Lockhart Elementary School
Tampa, Florida

Denise Kuhling
Adams Middle School
Tampa, Florida

Esther Leonard, M.Ed. and L.M.T.
Gifted and talented Implementation Specialist
San Antonio Independent School District
San Antonio, Texas

Kelly Maharaj
Challenger K–8 School of Science
 and Mathematics
Spring Hill, Florida

Kevin J. Maser, Ed.D.
H. Frank Carey Jr/Sr High School
Franklin Square, New York

Angie L. Matamoros, Ph.D.
ALM Science Consultant
Weston, Florida

Corey Mayle
Brogden Middle School
Durham, North Carolina

Keith McCarthy
George Washington Middle School
Wayne, New Jersey

Yolanda O. Peña
John F. Kennedy Junior High School
West Valley City, Utah

Kathleen M. Poe
Jacksonville Beach Elementary School
Jacksonville Beach, Florida

Wendy Rauld
Monroe Middle School
Tampa, Florida

Anne Rice
Woodland Middle School
Gurnee, Illinois

Bryna Selig
Gaithersburg Middle School
Gaithersburg, Maryland

Pat (Patricia) Shane, Ph.D.
STEM & ELA Education Consultant
Chapel Hill, North Carolina

Diana Shelton
Burnett Middle School
Seffner, Florida

Nakia Sturrup
Jennings Middle School
Seffner, Florida

Melissa Triebwasser
Walden Lake Elementary
Plant City, Florida

Michele Bubley Wiehagen
Science Coach
Miles Elementary School
Tampa, Florida

Pauline Wilcox
Instructional Science Coach
Fox Chapel Middle School
Spring Hill, Florida

Safety Reviewers

Douglas Mandt, M.S.
Science Education Consultant
Edgewood, Washington

Juliana Textley, Ph.D.
Author, NSTA books on school science safety
Adjunct Professor
Lesley University
Cambridge, Massachusetts

MS-LS3-1, MS-LS3-2, MS-LS4-4, MS-LS4-5

Go to PearsonRealize.com to access your digital course.

▶ **VIDEO**
  • Genetic Counselor

👆 **INTERACTIVITY**
  • Making Copies
  • Offspring Season
  • Look Inside
  • Colorful Chromosome
  • The Role of DNA
  • Making Proteins
  • Sex-Linked Traits and Disorders
  • Track Your Traits
  • DNA Fingerprinting
  • Solving Problems with Genetics

📱 **VIRTUAL LAB**
  • Whose Offspring is This?

☑ **ASSESSMENT**

📖 **eTEXT**

HANDS-ON LABS

Connect Making More

Investigate
  • Observing Pistils and Stamens
  • Chromosomes and Inheritance
  • Modeling Protein Synthesis
  • Extraction in Action

Demonstrate
Make the Right Call!

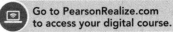

Go to PearsonRealize.com to access your digital course.

VIDEO
• Evolutionary Biologist

INTERACTIVITY
• Mystery on the Galapagos Islands
• Animal Feeding Adaptations
• Adaptations and Variations • Mice Selection on the Prairie • Species Adaptations • Lessons from the Potato Famine • Mutations Aren't All that Bad • Separated Species • Along the Canyon Wall • Legs, Arms, Wings, Flippers • Tiny Clues • Fossils Around the World • Tree of Life • Long Necks and Hoofed Feet

VIRTUAL LAB
• Natural Selection in Butterfly Behavior

ASSESSMENT

eTEXT

HANDS-ON LABS

Connect Fins and Limbs!
Investigate
• Nature at Work
• Variation in a Population
• Adaptations of Birds
• Finding Proof
• DNA Evidence

Demonstrate
A Bony Puzzle

Elevate your thinking!

Elevate Science takes science to a whole new level and lets you take ownership of your learning. Explore science in the world around you. Investigate how things work. Think critically and solve problems! *Elevate Science* helps you think like a scientist, so you're ready for a world of discoveries.

Explore Your World

Explore real-life scenarios with engaging Quests that dig into science topics around the world. You can:

- Solve real-world problems
- Apply skills and knowledge
- Communicate solutions

Make Connections

Elevate Science connects science to other subjects and shows you how to better understand the world through:

- Mathematics
- Reading and Writing
- Literacy

Quest KICKOFF

What do you think is causing Pleasant Pond to turn green?

In 2016, algal blooms turned bodies of water green and slimy in Florida, Utah, California, and 17 other states. These blooms put people and ecosystems in danger. Scientists, such as limnologists, are working to predict and prevent future algal blooms. In this problem-based Quest activity, you will investigate an algal bloom at a lake and determine its cause. In labs and digital activities, you will apply what you learn in each lesson to help you gather evidence to solve the mystery. With enough evidence, you will be able to identify what you believe is the cause of the algal bloom and present a solution in the Findings activity.

Math Toolbox
Graphing Population Changes

Ohio's Deer Population

Changes in a population over time, such as white-tailed deer in Ohio, can be displayed in a graph.

Deer Population Trends, 2000–2010

Year	Population (estimated)	Year	Population (estimated)
2000	525,000	2006	770,000
2001	560,000	2007	725,000
2002	620,000	2008	745,000
2003	670,000	2009	750,000
2004	715,000	2010	710,000
2005	720,000		

Relationships Use the data

800,000

READING CHECK Determine Central ideas
What adaptations might the giraffe have that help it survive in its environment?

Academic Vocabulary
Relate the term *decomposer* to the verb *compose*. What does it mean to compose something?

Build Skills for the Future

- Master the Engineering Design Process
- Apply critical thinking and analytical skills
- Learn about STEM careers

Focus on Inquiry

Case studies put you in the shoes of a scientist to solve real-world mysteries using real data. You will be able to:

- Analyze Data
- Test a hypothesis
- Solve the Case

Case Study

MS-LS2-1

THE CASE OF THE DISAPPEARING

Cerulean Warbler

The cerulean warbler is a small, migratory songbird named for its blue color. Cerulean warblers breed in eastern North America during the spring and summer. The warblers spend the winter months in the Andes Mountains of Colombia, Venezuela, Ecuador, and Peru in northern part of South America.

Enter the Lab

Hands-on experiments and virtual labs help you test ideas and show what you know in performance-based assessments. Scaffolded labs include:

- STEM Labs
- Design Your Own
- Open-ended Labs

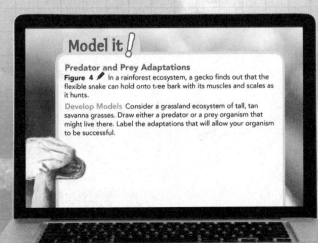

Model it!

Predator and Prey Adaptations

Figure 4 In a rainforest ecosystem, a gecko finds out that the flexible snake can hold onto tree bark with its muscles and scales as it hunts.

Develop Models Consider a grassland ecosystem of tall, tan savanna grasses. Draw either a predator or a prey organism that might live there. Label the adaptations that will allow your organism to be successful.

HANDS-ON LAB

Investigate Observe how once-living matter is broken down into smaller components in the process of decomposition.

Genes and Heredity

NGSS PERFORMANCE EXPECTATIONS

MS-LS3-1 Develop and use a model to describe why structural changes to genes (mutations) located on chromosomes may affect proteins and may result in harmful, beneficial, or neutral effects to the structure and function of the organism.

MS-LS3-2 Develop and use a model to describe why asexual reproduction results in offspring with identical genetic information and sexual reproduction results in offspring with genetic variation.

MS-LS4-4 Construct an explanation based on evidence that describes how genetic variations of traits in a population increase some individuals' probability of surviving and reproducing in a specific environment.

MS-LS4-5 Gather and synthesize information about the technologies that have changed the way humans influence the inheritance of desired traits in organisms.

HANDS-ON LAB

uConnect Explore the effects of
different methods of reproduction.

How can these horses be the parents of the foal?

GO ONLINE
to access your digital course

▶ VIDEO

☝ INTERACTIVITY

⏱ VIRTUAL LAB

☑ ASSESSMENT

📖 eTEXT

🧪 HANDS-ON LABS

The Essential Question

How do offspring receive traits from their parents?

CCC Cause and Effect You might expect a foal to look just like at least one parent, but offspring can vary greatly in appearance. How do you think this foal ended up looking so different from both parents?

....

....

....

....

....

Quest KICKOFF

How can you sell a new fruit?

Phenomenon Consumers are often open to new ideas—especially tasty new ideas. But it may take some convincing. What new fruit sensation can you develop, and how will you get growers and consumers to buy in? In this Quest activity, you will explore reproduction, heredity, and genetics as you choose desirable traits and figure out how to ensure their consistent appearance in your product. Once your new fruit is characterized, you will create a brochure to help growers understand your product, why it is desirable, and how they can grow it successfully.

NBC LEARN ▶ VIDEO

After watching the Quest Kickoff video about different kinds of fruit hybrids, think about the qualities you desire in your fruit. In the table below, identify the characteristics you want your new fruit to have.

Color	
Taste	
Size	
Shape	
Texture	

 INTERACTIVITY

Funky Fruits

MS-LS3-1 Develop and use a model to describe why structural changes to genes (mutations) located on chromosomes may affect proteins and may result in harmful, beneficial, or neutral effects to the structure and function of the organism.

MS-LS3-2 Develop and use a model to describe why asexual reproduction results in offspring with identical genetic information and sexual reproduction results in offspring with genetic variation.

MS-LS4-5 Gather and synthesize information about the technologies that have changed the way humans influence the inheritance of desired traits in organisms.

Quest CHECK-IN

IN LESSON 1

How can you use both sexual and asexual reproduction to develop your new fruit? Explore how farmers benefit from using both types of reproduction to establish and maintain a consistent product.

 INTERACTIVITY

An Apple Lesson

Quest CHECK-IN

IN LESSON 2

What role do chromosomes and genes play in fruit reproduction? Make a chromosome map and locate genes that carry desirable traits.

 INTERACTIVITY

About Those Chromosomes

IN LESSON 3

What do DNA and protein synthesis have to do with the traits exhibited by an organism? Consider how genes will affect the characteristics of your fruit.

These white strawberries, called pineberries, taste somewhat like pineapples.

Quest FINDINGS

Complete the Quest!

Create a brochure for prospective growers of your new fruit. Convince readers that your fruit will be a delicious success!

 INTERACTIVITY

Reflect on Funky Fruits

Quest CHECK-IN

IN LESSON 4

How are dominant and recessive traits inherited? Examine data tables for trait inheritance and complete Punnett squares to determine the probable outcomes of crosses.

HANDS-ON LAB

All in the Numbers

IN LESSON 5

How do growers ensure consistency in their product? Consider how you might use genetic technologies to develop your new fruit.

Making More

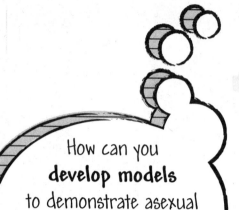

How can you **develop models** to demonstrate asexual reproduction and sexual reproduction?

Background

Phenomenon Organisms must reproduce, or make more of their own species, in order for the species to survive. There are different ways to reproduce, asexually or sexually. Asexually reproducing populations only require one parent and results in offspring with identical genetic information. Sexually reproducing populations require two parents and result in offspring with genetic variation. In this activity, you will develop models to demonstrate asexual reproduction and sexual reproduction.

Develop Models

(per group)
- bowl
- stopwatch (optional)
- paper plate
- dried beans
- graph paper

☐ 1. Use all of the materials. As you develop your model you should:
- Use the beans to represent the reproducing species.
- Consider the characteristics of each bean when selecting which one(s) will best help you represent your two models of reproduction.
- Set an amount of time for one reproductive cycle to occur.
- Collect quantitative data about the two populations of beans.

☐ 2. Describe how you will model asexual reproduction.

....
....
....
....

☐ 3. Describe how you will model sexual reproduction.

....
....
....
....

☐ 4. When you are done, use the graph paper to make a graph that shows the number of beans in each model.

Data and Observations

Asexual Reproduction	Sexual Reproduction

Analyze and Conclude

HANDS-ON LAB

ⓋConnect Go online for a downloadable worksheet of this lab.

1. **SEP Interpret Data** Which type of reproduction had the most beans at the end? Why?

   ....
   ....
   ....

2. **SEP Develop Models** Explain why you chose the bean(s) you did for the asexual reproduction model.

   ....
   ....

3. **SEP Develop Models** Explain why you chose the bean(s) you did for the sexual reproduction model.

   ....
   ....

4. **SEP Construct Explanations** Explain why the number of beans laid down by the asexual reproduction model should grow at least twice as fast. Why do you think asexual populations are not common in nature? Explain.

   ....
   ....
   ....
   ....

Patterns of Inheritance

Guiding Questions

- How did Gregor Mendel advance the fields of genetics and inheritance?
- How are inherited alleles related to an organism's traits?
- How is probability related to inheritance?

Connections

Literacy Determine Conclusions

Math Use a Probability Model

MS-LS3-2

uInvestigate Explore cross-pollination by examining the parts of a flower.

Vocabulary

heredity
dominant allele
recessive allele
probability
genotype
phenotype

Academic Vocabulary

quantify
factor

Connect It!

🖊 **Male northern cardinals express the trait for bright red feather color. Circle the male cardinal.**

Predict 🖊 List four more visible characteristics that these birds will pass on to their offspring. Then list the inherited trait that their offspring will possess.

Visible Characteristics	Inherited Traits
reddish bill color	bill color

CCC Patterns Will their offspring look exactly like the parents? Explain.

....

....

Mendel's Observations

Like all other organisms, the cardinals in **Figure 1** pass their traits to their offspring. To better understand **heredity**, the passing of traits from parents to offspring, it is important to learn about the history behind the science. In the 1800s, a European monk named Gregor Mendel studied heredity. Mendel's job at the monastery was to tend the garden. After several years of growing pea plants, he became very familiar with seven possible traits the plants could have. Some plants grew tall, while others were short. Some produced green seeds, while others produced yellow.

Mendel's Experiments

Mendel's studies became some of the most important in biology because he was one of the first to **quantify** his results. He collected, recorded, and analyzed data from the thousands of tests that he ran.

The experiments Mendel performed involved transferring the male flower part of a pea plant to the female flower part to get a desired trait. Mendel wanted to see what would happen with pea plants when he crossed different traits: short and tall, yellow seeds and green seeds, and so on. Because of his detailed work with heredity, Mendel is often referred to as the "father of modern genetics."

HANDS-ON LAB

Explore how human height is inherited.

Academic Vocabulary

In Latin, *quantus* means "how much." Have you heard the word quantify used before? Does it remind you of any other words?

....

....

....

....

....

....

Passing on Traits
Figure 1 Male and female northern cardinals share many traits, but also have several that make them unique.

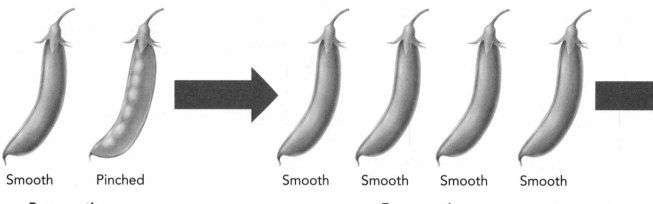

Smooth   Pinched
P generation

Smooth   Smooth   Smooth   Smooth
F₁ generation

Pea Pod Shape

Figure 2 ✏ Circle the pod shape in the P generation that has the dominant trait.

Parents and Offspring When Mendel cross-pollinated, or crossed, a tall plant with a short one, all of the offspring were tall. The tall plant and short plant that were crossed are called the parent plants, or P generation. The offspring are called the F_1, or first filial generation. The term *filial* originates from the Latin terms *filius* and *filia*, which mean "son" and "daughter," respectively.

Mendel examined several traits of pea plants. Through his experimentation, he realized that certain patterns formed. When a plant with green peas was crossed with one with yellow peas, all of the F_1 offspring were yellow. However, when he crossed these offspring, creating what is called the second filial generation, or F_2, the resulting offspring were not all yellow. For every four offspring, three were yellow and one was green. This pattern of inheritance appeared repeatedly when Mendel tested other traits, such as pea pod shape shown in **Figure 2**. Mendel concluded that while only one form of the trait is visible in F_1, in F_2 the missing trait sometimes shows itself.

Plan It

SEP Plan Investigations Consider five other traits that Mendel investigated. Explain how you could repeat Mendel's procedure for one of these traits and what the likely results would be of your investigation.

Trait	Dominant	Recessive
seed shape	round	wrinkled
seed color	yellow	green
pod color	green	yellow
flower color	purple	white
pod position on stem	side of stem	top of stem

....

....

....

....

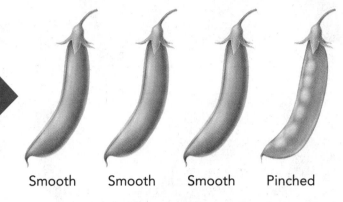

Smooth   Smooth   Smooth   Pinched

F$_2$ generation

INTERACTIVITY

Examine different methods of passing on genes to offspring.

HANDS-ON LAB

Investigate Explore cross-pollination by examining the parts of a flower.

Alleles Affect Inheritance

In Mendel's time, people had no knowledge of genetic material or its ability to carry the code for an organism's traits. However, Mendel was still able to formulate several ideas about heredity from his experiments. He called the information that carried the traits **factors**, because they determined what was expressed. He also determined that for every trait, organisms receive one factor from their mother and one factor from their father. He concluded that one factor can mask the expression of the other even if both are present at the same time.

Genes and Alleles Today, the term *factor* has been replaced with *gene* or *allele*. Alleles are the different forms of a gene. Pea plants have one gene that controls the color of the seeds. This gene may express itself as being either yellow or green through a combination of yellow alleles and green alleles. When crossed, each parent donates one of its alleles for seed color to the offspring. The allele that each parent donates is random. An offspring's seed color is determined by the combination of both alleles.

An organism's traits are controlled by the alleles it inherits. A **dominant allele** is one whose trait always shows up in the organism when the allele is present. A **recessive allele**, on the other hand, is hidden whenever the dominant allele is present. If one parent donates a dominant allele and the other donates a recessive allele, only the dominant trait will be expressed.

✓ READING CHECK **Determine Conclusions** What conditions would have to occur for an offspring to express the recessive trait?

....

....

Academic Vocabulary

How is factor used differently in math and science?

....

....

....

....

....

....

Reflect Think about a time when you saw a baby animal, such as a puppy or kitten. Think about the traits it inherited from its parents. How could you determine which traits were dominant and which where recessive? Discuss the question with a classmate and record your ideas in your science notebook.

Dominating Color

Figure 3 ✏ Mendel discovered that yellow is the dominant pea seed color, while recessive pea seed color is green. Complete the statements. Use the letters G and g as needed.

Apply Concepts What are the alleles for the green pea seed? Would it be a pure-bred or a hybrid?

....

....

The alleles for a purebred yellow seed would be ....

The alleles for a hybrid yellow seed would be ....

Literacy Connection

Determine Conclusions How did Mendel come to the conclusion that an organism's traits were carried on different alleles? Underline the sentence that answers this question.

Writing Alleles The traits we see are present because of the combination of alleles. For example, the peas in **Figure 3** show two different colors. Pea color is the gene, while the combinations of alleles determines how the gene will be expressed. To represent this, scientists who study patterns of inheritance, called geneticists, use letters to represent the alleles. A dominant allele is represented with a capital letter (G) and a recessive allele with a lowercase letter (g).

When an organism has two of the same alleles for a trait, it is called a purebred. This would be represented as GG or gg. When the organism has one dominant allele and one recessive allele, it is called a hybrid. This would be represented as Gg. Remember that each trait is represented by two alleles, one from the mother and one from the father. Depending upon which alleles are inherited, the offspring may be a purebred or a hybrid.

Mendel's work was quite revolutionary. Prior to his work, many people assumed that all traits in offspring were a mixture of each parent's traits. Mendel's experiments, where traits appeared in the F_2 generation that were not in the F_1 generation, disproved this idea.

Probability and Heredity

When you flip a coin, what are the chances it will come up heads? Because there are two options (heads or tails), the probability of getting heads is 1 out of 2. The coin has an equal chance of coming up heads or tails. Each toss has no effect on the outcome of the next toss. **Probability** is a number that describes how likely it is that an event will occur. The laws of probability predict what is likely to happen and what is not likely to happen.

Probability and Genetics When dealing with genetics and inheritance, it is important to know the laws of probability. Every time two parents produce offspring, the probability of certain traits getting passed on is the same. For example, do you know any families that have multiple children, but all of them are the same sex? Picture a family where all the children are girls. According to the laws of probability, a boy should have been born already, but there is no guarantee of that happening. Every time these parents have a child, the probability of having a boy remains the same as the probability of having a girl.

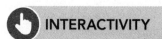

INTERACTIVITY

Collect data to determine whether a trait is genetic or acquired.

Math Toolbox

Determining Probability

Probability is an important part of the science of genetics. Answer the questions on probability below.

1. Predict The probability of a specific allele from one parent being passed on to an offspring is 1 in 2, or ½. This is the same probability as predicting a coin toss correctly. How often would you expect a coin to show tails if you flip it 100 times?

....

2. SEP Identify Patterns A die is a six-sided cube with dots representing the numbers 1 through 6. What is the probability of rolling a 3?

....

3. Use a Probability Model You and a friend both roll a die at the same time. On the first roll, the dots on the two dice add up to 7. On the second roll, they add up to 2. Which do you think was more likely, rolling a total of 2 or a total of 7? Explain your answer.

....

....

....

....

▶ **VIDEO**

Further examine the process of making a Punnett square.

Making a Punnett Square

To determine the probability of inheriting alleles, geneticists use a tool called a Punnett square. To construct a Punnett square, it is important to know what trait is being considered and whether the parents are purebred or hybrid.

The following steps demonstrate how to use a Punnett square to calculate the probability of offspring having different combinations of alleles. The example describes the procedure for a cross between two hybrid parents; however, this procedure will work for any cross.

Using a Punnett Square

Mendel's experiments involved crossing two hybrid pea plants in the F_1 generation. Most plants in the F_2 generation showed the dominant trait, but some showed the recessive trait. A Punnett square uses the laws of probability to demonstrate why those results occurred. Consider the question of what the offspring of two hybrid pea plants with yellow seed color will be.

1 **Draw a square box** divided into four square parts.

One parent's alleles go on top and the other parent's alleles go on the left.

2 **Determine the alleles** of each of the parents. You know that they are both hybrids, so they have one dominant allele (represented as a capital letter) and one recessive allele (represented as a lowercase letter). Place one set of alleles on top of the columns of the box, and one set of alleles next to the rows of the box, as shown.

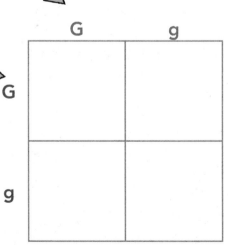

3 **Do the cross!** Inside each box, combine the letter at the top of the column with the letter to the left of the row the box is in. Always write a dominant allele before a recessive allele.

	G	g
G	GG	Gg
g	Gg	gg

4 **Determine the likelihood** of different combinations of alleles. As you can see from the Punnett square, the combination GG occurs ¼ of the time, the combination Gg occurs ²⁄₄, or ½ of the time, and the combination gg occurs ¼ of the time.

5 **Determine which trait is expressed** for each combination of alleles. In this example, the combination GG and Gg result in the dominant yellow seed color, while the combination gg results in the green seed color. Therefore, the dominant allele will be expressed ¾ of the time. This matches the results of Mendel's experiments.

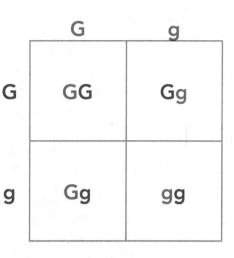

SEP Use Models ✏ You cross a pea plant that is hybrid for yellow seed color (Gg) with a purebred green seed color (gg) plant. Draw a Punnett square to show the results of the cross. What is the probability that the offspring will have green seed color?

....

INTERACTIVITY

Use models to describe how sexual reproduction leads to genetic variation.

Genotype

You are already familiar with the terms *purebred* and *hybrid*. These terms refer to **genotype**, an organism's genetic makeup or combination of alleles. As shown in **Figure 4**, the genotype of a purebred green seed pea plant would be gg. Both alleles are the same (purebred) and they are recessive because green is the recessive trait in terms of seed color. The hybrid genotype for this trait would be Gg.

The expression of an organism's genes is called its **phenotype**, the organism's physical appearance or visible traits. The height, the shape, the color, the size, the texture—whatever trait is being expressed, is referred to as the phenotype. So, a pea plant with the phenotype of yellow seed color could have two possible genotypes, GG or Gg.

Genotypes and Phenotypes for Seed Color

Figure 4 The phenotype of an organism is explained as physical characteristics we see, while the genotype describes the combination of alleles that are inherited.

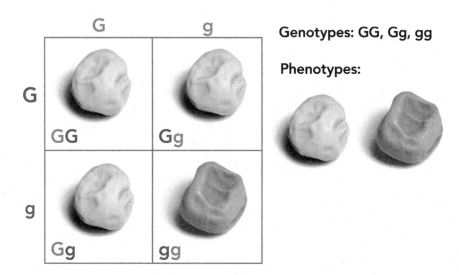

There are two other terms geneticists use to describe genotypes. Instead of saying purebred, they refer to an organism with two identical alleles as homozygous (*homo-* means "the same"). When the alleles are both dominant, as in the yellow seed plant (GG), the genotype is called homozygous dominant. However, when the alleles are both recessive, as in the green seed color (gg), the genotype is called homozygous recessive. When an organism is a hybrid, as in yellow seed color (Gg), the genotype is called the heterozygous condition (*hetero-* means "different").

☑ READING CHECK **Determine Differences**
Explain how genotypes and phenotypes are different.

....

....

1. **Apply Concepts** The dominant allele for dimples is *D* and the recessive allele is *d*. How would a geneticist describe the genotype of an individual with the alleles *dd*?

....

Use the information you calculated in the Punnett square activity to answer questions 2 and 3.

2. **SEP Interpret Data** How did the probabilities of yellow seeds and green seeds compare with each other?

....
....
....
....

3. **CCC Cause and Effect** What would happen to the probabilities of yellow and green seeds if one parent were homozygous recessive and the other were homozygous dominant?

....
....
....
....

4. **SEP Construct an Explanation** Why were Mendel's experiments with pea plants so important toward advancing current knowledge of genetics and inheritance?

....
....
....
....
....
....

5. **Predict** For plant stem length, the dominant allele for height is T and the recessive allele is t. What would be the genotypes, phenotypes, and offspring probabilities of a cross between a heterozygous parent for tall stem length and one that was homozygous recessive for short stem length?

....
....
....
....
....

Quest CHECK-IN

In this lesson, you learned how inherited alleles determine traits and how probability is related to inheritance. You also explored the factors that determine an organism's genotype and phenotype.

SEP Design Solutions How can you increase the likelihood that the desired trait will be inherited in your fruit?

....
....
....

👆 INTERACTIVITY

An Apple Lesson

Go online to explore how you can utilize both sexual and asexual reproduction to develop your new fruit.

MS-LS3-1, MS-LS3-2, MS-LS4-4

CEPHALOPODS

SPECIAL EDITION

Octopuses, squids, and cuttlefish are a type of mollusk called cephalopods. These soft-bodied invertebrates reproduce sexually. They are fast swimmers and aggressive predators.

With prominent heads and multiple tentacles, cephalopods are known for their complex behaviors and for being extremely intelligent.

Cephalopods also have a remarkably large genome— it's even larger than the human genome! Their genome stands out because it has many genes related to neuron connectivity, which might explain their unusually large brains and intelligence. Cephalopods are so smart that they can solve puzzles, use tools, and even open jars.

Adding Variation

Sexual reproduction is not the only process that contributes to making offspring different from their parents. Squids and octopuses, for example, have developed a clever mechanism that increases variation in traits without really having to make changes to their genetic information.

Some genetic information becomes traits by means of a messenger molecule called RNA. RNA is the molecule that allows the expression of genetic information.

In a process called RNA editing, squids and octopuses can make changes to RNA, the messenger molecule. RNA editing leads to a change in traits that are expressed, regardless of the information coded in the genome. The highest rate of RNA-editing takes place in nervous system cells.

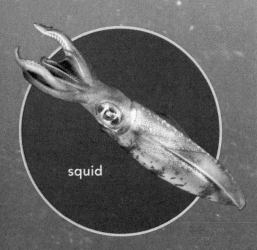

squid

octopus

RNA editing in cephalopods is triggered by environmental factors. It could be turned on when the cephalopod travels from the tropics from the arctic. Or it will turn off the RNA editing when the cephalopod remains in one location.

One fascinating feature of RNA editing is that not all of the messenger molecules are edited the same way. As a result, many different RNA messenger molecules can come out of one single gene.

cuttlefish

Scientists think that this increase in variation may also explain cephalopods' complex brains and high intelligence. They also wonder whether there could be a trade off. By relying on RNA editing to adapt to such influences in the environment as temperature changes and experiences, could these special cephalopods be losing something else? After all, these specific changes are not passed down to their offspring.

Read the case study and answer the following questions.

1. **SEP Analyze Data** Suppose the ability to edit RNA is a dominant trait. A male squid with two dominant alleles for RNA editing sexually reproduces with a female squid that has two recessive alleles for RNA editing. Will their offspring be able to edit their RNA? Explain.

   ....

2. **SEP Evaluate Information** If there is a change in a squid's messenger RNA, will this change appear in its genetic material? Will it be inherited by its offspring?

   ....

   ....

3. **SEP Construct Explanations** How can changes in RNA be beneficial for squids?

   ....

   ....

4. **CCC Structure and Function** What do you think could happen if humans had the same RNA-editing ability as cephalopods? What might be the result?

   ....

   ....

   ....

Chromosomes and Inheritance

Guiding Questions

- What is the relationship among genes, chromosomes, and inheritance?
- How is a pedigree used to track inheritance?
- How does the formation of sex cells during meiosis differ from the process of cell division?

Connections

Literacy Read and Comprehend

Math Model With Mathematics

MS-LS3-2

HANDS-ON LAB

uInvestigate Investigate genetic crosses in imaginary creatures.

Vocabulary

chromosome
cell cycle
pedigree
meiosis
chromatids
mitosis

Academic Vocabulary

structure
function

Connect It!

🖊 **Circle the traits that are similar between the parents and the offspring.**

Apply Concepts How were the traits transferred from the parents to the ducklings during reproduction? Where were those traits found?

....

....

....

CCC Cause and Effect Each duckling came from these parents. They look similar, but they are not exactly the same. Why are they not identical? Explain.

....

....

Chromosomes and Genes

Gregor Mendel's ideas about inheritance and probability can be applied to all living things. Mendel determined that traits are inherited using pieces of information that he called factors and we call genes. He observed and experimented with genes in pea plants. He discovered how genes, such as those in ducks (**Figure 1**), were transferred from parents to offspring and how they made certain traits appear. However, Mendel did not know what genes actually look like.

Today, scientists know that genes are segments of code that appear on structures called **chromosomes**. These threadlike **structures** within a cell's nucleus contain DNA that is passed from one generation to the next. These threadlike strands of genetic material have condensed and wrapped themselves around special proteins. This provides support for the chromosome structure.

Chromosomes are made in the beginning of the **cell cycle**, the series of events in which a cell grows, prepares for division, and divides to form daughter cells. During this time, the chromosome gets its characteristic *X* shape.

Academic Vocabulary

Identify and describe something that has a particular structure.

....

....

....

....

....

Parents Pass Traits to Their Offspring
Figure 1 Each baby mallard duck receives some traits from the mother and some from the father.

17

Scales of Genetic Material

Figure 2 ✎ Order the structures from smallest to largest by writing the numbers 1 through 5 in the blank circles. Number 1 is the smallest.

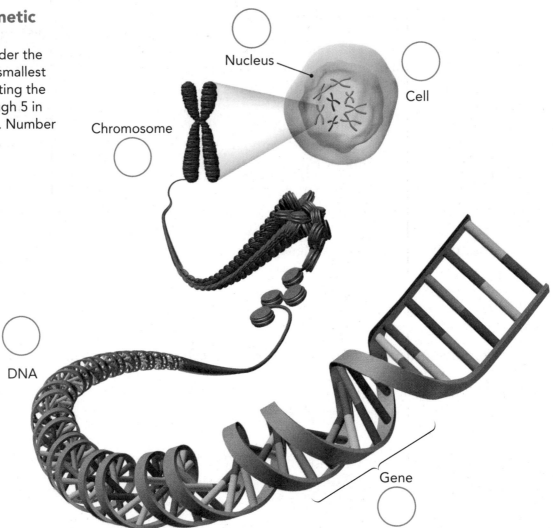

Nucleus

Cell

Chromosome

DNA

Gene

📓 **Make Meaning** Why do sex cells contain only half the number of chromosomes needed for offspring? In your science notebook, explain what would happen if sex cells contained the same number of chromosomes as body cells.

Academic Vocabulary

What is the difference between an object's structure and its function?

....

....

....

Number of Chromosomes Every cell in your body other than the sex cells has the same number of chromosomes. In humans, this number is 46. Other organisms have different numbers of chromosomes, and there is a great variety. For example, mallard ducks have 80 chromosomes. All sexually-reproducing organisms form sex cells, which have half the number of chromosomes that body cells have.

Genes on Chromosomes Every living thing needs instructions to live. Without these instructions, living things would not be able to grow and **function**. These instructions are located on genes. As you can see in **Figure 2,** genes are located on chromosomes.

In humans, between 20,000 and 25,000 genes are found on the 46 chromosomes. Chromosomes are different sizes. Larger chromosomes contain more genes than smaller chromosomes. Each gene contains instructions for coding a particular trait. There are hundreds to thousands of genes coding traits on any given chromosome. For many organisms, these chromosomes come in sets.

Chromosome Pairs During fertilization, you receive 23 chromosomes from your father and 23 chromosomes from your mother. These chromosomes come in pairs, called homologous chromosomes, that contain the same genes. Two alleles—one from the mother and one from the father—represent each trait. However, the alleles for these genes may or may not be the same. Some of the alleles for how the gene is expressed may be dominant or recessive. In **Figure 3**, the offspring that received these chromosomes inherited two different forms of a gene—allele *A* from one parent and allele *a* from the other. The individual will be heterozygous for that gene trait. Because more than one gene is present on the 23 pairs of chromosomes, there is a wide variety of allele combinations.

✓ READING CHECK **Integrate with Visuals** How would geneticists—people who study genes—know whether the organism in **Figure 3** is homozygous or heterozygous for a certain trait by examining the chromosome pair?

....

....

....

....

Chromosome pair

A Pair of Chromosomes

Figure 3 🖊 Circle all the pairs of alleles that would be homozygous for a trait.

Counting on Chromosomes

1. **SEP Model with Mathematics** 🖊 Fill in the table with the appropriate chromosome number for the missing body cell or sex cell.

Organisms	Number of Chromosomes	
	Body Cells	Sex Cells
House cat	38	
Mallard duck		40
Corn	20	
Peanut	40	
Horse		32
Oak tree		12
Sweet potato	90	
Camel		35
Chicken	78	

2. **Construct Graphs** 🖊 Complete the line plot below. Place an *X* for each organism whose body cell chromosome number falls within the given range.

Body Cell Chromosome Distribution

| 0–20 | 21–40 | 41–60 | 61–80 | 81–100 |

Number of chromosomes

Tracking Traits

Figure 4 Sickle cell anemia is a genetic disease that changes the structure of red blood cells. In the pedigree, affected members are shaded.

1. Claim 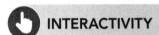 Circle couples on the pedigree who are both carriers for the trait.

2. Evidence What is your proof?

....

....

3. Reasoning Explain how your evidence supports your claim.

....

....

....

....

INTERACTIVITY

Take a look inside the formation of sex cells through meiosis.

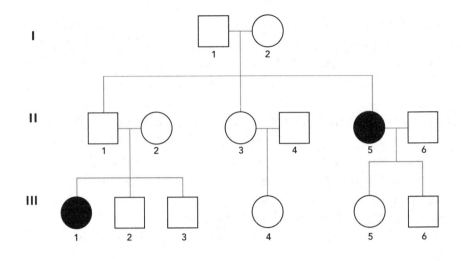

Using a Pedigree

Alelles can sometimes recombine to produce traits that are not favorable, such as a genetic disease. Geneticists study how traits are inherited in order to trace their genetic origin and predict how they may be passed on to future generations.

A **pedigree** is a tool that geneticists use to map out the inheritance of traits. The diagram shows the presence or absence of a trait according to the relationships within a family across several generations. It is like a family tree. **Figure 4** shows multiple generations represented by Roman numerals I, II, and III. Most pedigrees show which family members express a particular trait (shaded figures) as well as the individuals who carry the trait but do not express it (half-shaded figures). In a pedigree, males are represented with squares and females with circles. One horizontal line connects the parent couple and another line leads down from the parents to their children.

 Model It

SEP Develop Models 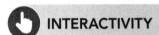 Think of a trait that you admire. How can that trait get passed through a family? Create a pedigree that outlines the transmission of this trait through a family. Consider who has the trait, who is a carrier for it, and who does not have it.

Forming Sex Cells

In an organism that is reproduced sexually, a body cell has twice as many chromosomes a sex cell. Why is this important? Well, it is through the sex cells that parents pass their genes on to their offspring. When the sperm and egg fuse, they form a zygote, or fertilized egg. The zygote gets two sets of chromosomes—one set from the sperm and one set from the egg. Human eggs, for example, contain 23 total chromosomes in a set and sperm contain 23 total chromosomes in a set. So, each of your body cells contains one set of chromosomes from your mother and another set from your father for a total of 46 chromosomes.

Sex cells (sperm and egg) are formed through a very specialized process called **meiosis**, during which the number of chromosomes is reduced by half. It is through meiosis that homologous chromosomes separate into two different cells. This creates new cells with half as many chromosomes as the parent cell.

Homologous chromosomes have one chromosome from each parent. While the two chromosomes share the same sequence of genes, they may have different alleles. Before the chromosomes separate and move into separate cells, they undergo a process called crossing over. Notice in **Figure 5** that a small segment of one chromosome exchanges places with the corresponding segment on the other chromosome. By exchanging this genetic information, the new cells that form will have a slightly different combination of genes. This allows for minor variations in traits to form, which means there is a higher likelihood that offspring with desirable traits will form within the larger population.

Swapping Genetic Material

Figure 5 ✏ During crossing over, a segment of the gene from the mother changes places with a segment of the same gene from the father. Circle the gene segments that exchanged places.

CCC Cause and Effect What would happen to offspring if crossing over did not occur during the first part of meiosis?

....

....

....

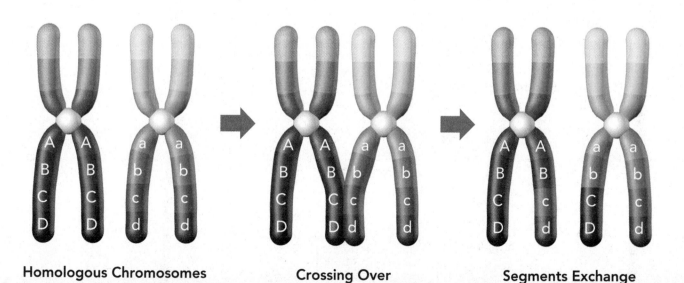

Homologous Chromosomes   Crossing Over   Segments Exchange

VIDEO

Observe the process of meiosis in action.

INTERACTIVITY

Trace the path of a particular trait through meiosis.

Meiosis Before a cell can divide, the genetic material condenses into chromosomes. **Figure 6** shows how meiosis starts with the genetic material being copied and condensing into chromosomes. After crossing over, the chromosomes separate and the cell divides into two cells. Each new cell, now containing half the number of chromosomes, then divides again, making a total of four daughter cells. Meiosis II in **Figure 6** shows how this second division occurs. Each chromosome splits into two rod-like structures called **chromatids**. Each chromatid contains a double helix of DNA. Note that each of the four daughter cells has one distinct chromatid.

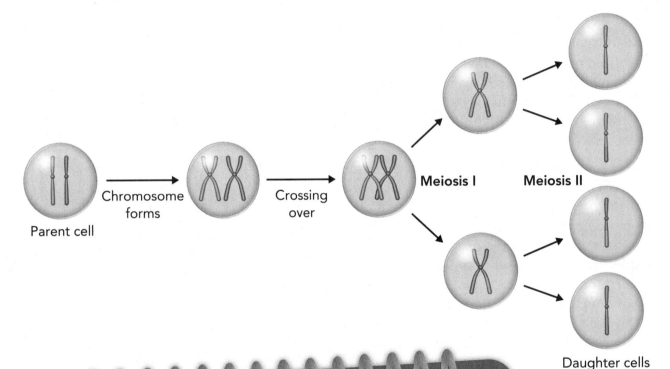

Parent cell — Chromosome forms — Crossing over — **Meiosis I** — **Meiosis II** — Daughter cells

Meiosis
Figure 6 The process of meiosis forms sex cells.

1. **SEP Use Models** How is the genetic material of the parent cell different from the four cells that are formed?

....

....

2. **Sequence** ✏ Order the events of meiosis correctly.

_____ Four daughter cells are formed.

_____ Chromosome splits into two chromatids.

_____ Chromosome pairs come together and cross over.

_____ Cell divides into two daughter cells.

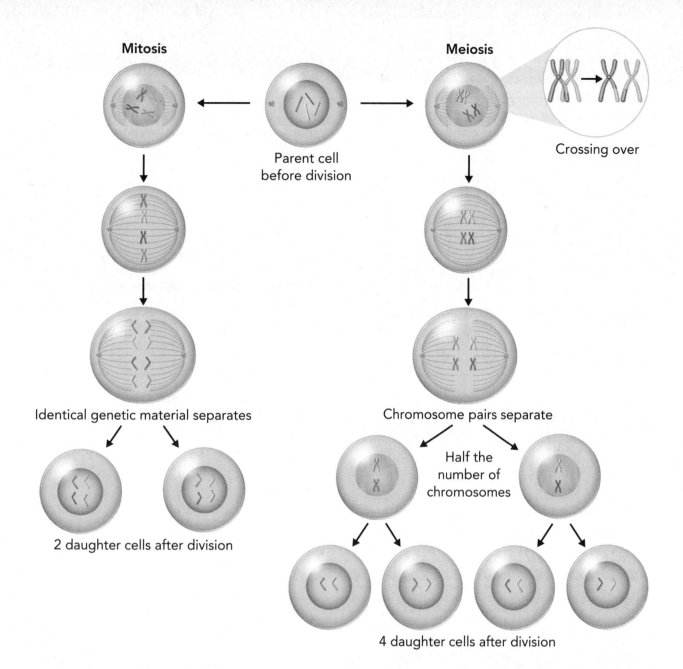

Mitosis

Parent cell before division

Meiosis

Crossing over

Identical genetic material separates

2 daughter cells after division

Chromosome pairs separate

Half the number of chromosomes

4 daughter cells after division

Comparing Meiosis and Mitosis The two main types of cell division are meiosis and mitosis. The majority of our body cells divide to make two genetically identical new cells in a process called **mitosis**: The cell's nucleus divides into two new nuclei, and identical copies of the parent cell's genetic material are distributed into each daughter cell.

Compare the processes of meiosis and mitosis shown in **Figure 7**. Mitosis produces two identical daughter cells with the same DNA as the parent cell. The sex cells produced by meiosis, however, are not genetically identical. There are two reasons for this difference. First, crossing over exchanges genetic material between homologous chromosomes. Secondly, the two cell divisions that occur in meiosis produce four daughter cells and each cell has half its parent cell's DNA. As a result, each sex cell has different genetic information.

Meiosis versus Mitosis
Figure 7 While meiosis forms sex cells, mitosis forms new body cells.

☑LESSON 2 Check

Use the pedigree to answer questions 1 & 2.

In humans, free earlobes are dominant and attached earlobes are recessive. The pedigree shows the transmission of attached earlobes through four generations of a family.

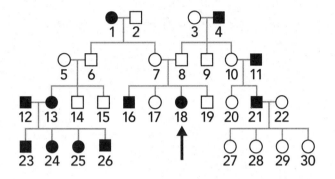

1. SEP Use Models Which male members of the family have attached earlobes?

....

2. Predict If the female marked by the arrow (individual 18) has a child with a male carrier, what is the probability their child will have attached earlobes?

....

3. SEP Provide Evidence Is chromosome number a good predictor of organism complexity? Explain.

....
....
....
....

4. SEP Use Mathematics A male king crab has 104 chromosomes in a sperm cell. How many chromosomes does it have in each of its body cells?

....

5. CCC Cause and Effect How can crossing over lead to the expression of new traits?

....
....
....
....
....

Quest CHECK-IN

In this lesson you learned how chromosomes carry genes and how chromosomes come in pairs that you receive from each parent. You explored how combinations of alleles are passed down in families. You also learned how cells can divide to create genetically similar cells or to create sex cells.

Apply Concepts A domestic cat has 38 chromosomes in its skin cells, while a dog has 78 chromosomes. How does this fact help to explain why dogs and cats cannot interbreed?

....
....
....

⏱ INTERACTIVITY

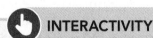

Go online to begin your chromosome map.

CAREERS
Genetic Counselor

Chromosome
COUNSELORS

S ometimes it runs in the family, as they say. We get traits such as eye color from genes passed on to us by our parents, but we can inherit diseases, too.

Genetic counselors help people who are at risk for a disease or a genetic disorder. Thexy are experts in genetics, so they know better than anyone how genes work. And they are trained counselors, too. They give emotional support and help families make health decisions.

For example, a genetic counselor might help new parents of a baby with Down syndrome. Or the counselor might meet with a patient whose family has a history of Alzheimer's.

Genetic counselors study a family's health history, order genetic tests, and help people to live with a genetic disease. They even advise doctors. They're the genetic experts, and they share their knowledge to help people.

Genetic counselors complete a four-year bachelor's degree in biology or a healthcare field. After graduating, they work on completing a master's degree. This degree will focus on human genetics and counseling. They also complete extensive research. In addition, excellent communication and decision-making skills are required.

▶ VIDEO

Watch what's involved with being a genetic counselor.

MY CAREER

Want to help people understand their genes? Do an online search for "genetic counselor" to learn more about this career.

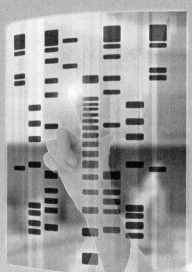

Phenomenon Genetic counselors help others understand the complex world of DNA, genes, and chromosomes.

25

3 Genetic Coding and Protein Synthesis

Guiding Questions

- Why do cells undergo DNA replication?
- How do cells make proteins?
- Why do cells undergo protein synthesis?

Connection

Literacy Draw Comparative Inferences

MS-LS3-1

HANDS-ON LAB

uInvestigate Make a model of the process of protein synthesis.

Vocabulary	Academic Vocabulary
DNA	sequence
protein synthesis	
messenger RNA	
transfer RNA	

Connect It!

✎ **A blueprint is a plan to build something. Circle the blueprint.**

Make Connections When have you used instructions to build something?

....

....

SEP Designing Solutions How did the instructions help you with building the structure?

....

....

The Genetic Code

Just as the couple in **Figure 1** need a blueprint to renovate a house, your body needs a plan to carry out daily functions. Your "blueprint" is found in the nucleus of each cell in the form of **DNA**. DNA (deoxyribonucleic acid) is the genetic material that carries information about an organism and is passed from parent to offspring.

In 1953, almost 100 years after DNA was discovered, scientists realized that DNA was shaped like a double helix—a twisted ladder. The structure of DNA consists of sugars, phosphates, and nitrogen bases. The sides of the ladder are made of sugar molecules, called deoxyribose, alternating with phosphate molecules. The rungs of the ladder are made of nitrogen bases. DNA has four nitrogen bases: adenine (A), thymine (T), guanine (G), and cytosine (C).

Genes are sections of DNA found on chromosomes. Each gene consists of hundreds or thousands of nitrogen bases arranged in a **sequence**. And it's this order that forms the instructions for building proteins — long chains of amino acids. Genes direct the construction of proteins, which in turn affect the traits that individuals receive from their parent(s). In other words, proteins trigger cellular processes that determine how inherited traits get expressed.

INTERACTIVITY

Explore the role of DNA in cellular processes and reproduction.

Academic Vocabulary

List some other contexts in which you have seen the word sequence.

....

....

....

....

....

Using a Blueprint

Figure 1 A blueprint is a plan for a building. DNA is the blueprint for constructing an organism.

Making Copies

Figure 2 ✎ In the circles, label the five nitrogen bases that would pair with the bases between the two arrows on the bottom strand.

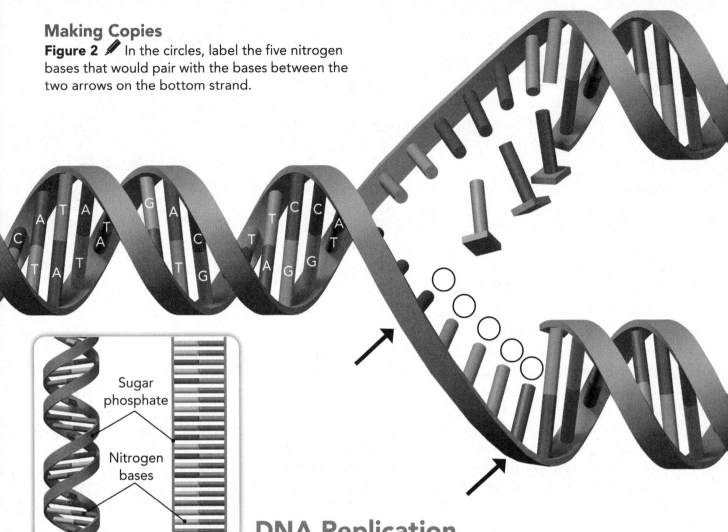

Sugar
phosphate

Nitrogen
bases

▶ **VIDEO**

Learn how the simplicity of DNA's four-letter code leads to the complexity of life.

DNA Replication

Scientists estimate that humans are made of approximately 37 trillion cells. As you grow and age, new cells form to build and repair structures or to replace cells that have died. For this to happen, cells need to replicate, and this requires making copies of DNA.

As shown in **Figure 2**, DNA replication begins when the double helix untwists. Then, a protein breaks the DNA strand in half—at the structure's weakest point—between the nitrogen bases. This separation actually looks like a zipper (**Figure 3**), and is often referred to as "unzipping the DNA." Next, nitrogen bases with a sugar and phosphate attached pair up with the bases on each half of the DNA. Because nitrogen bases always pair in the same way, adenine with thymine and guanine with cytosine, the order of the bases on both strands are identical. At the end of replication, a chromosome with two identical DNA strands is formed.

☑ READING CHECK **Cite Textual Evidence** How is the separation of DNA like a zipper?

....

....

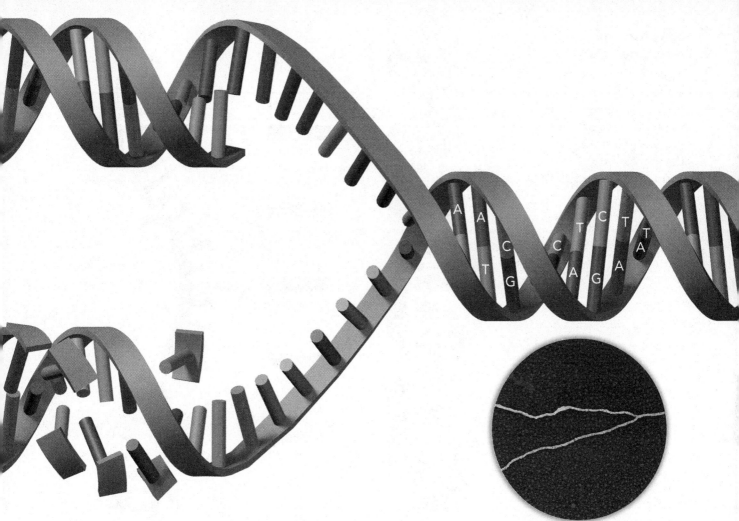

The process of DNA replication, or copying, ensures that each chromatid of a chromosome has identical DNA. During cell division, chromosomes split. During mitosis, the identical chromatids separate, resulting in identical DNA in each daughter cell. During meiosis, crossing over occurs before the chromatids split. No matter the type of cell division, DNA replication ensures that each cell contains the correct amount of DNA to carry out life processes.

Magnified Strand of DNA

Figure 3 This photograph taken by an electron microscope shows DNA replication in action.

Design It !

SEP Develop Models ✏ Sketch how you would model DNA replication using household materials such as beads and pipe cleaners. How do the pipe cleaners and beads relate to the structure and function of DNA?

Structure of DNA and RNA

Figure 4 Differences between DNA and RNA are apparent when comparing their structure. Use the diagram to identify two differences between a DNA molecule and an RNA molecule.

....

....

....

....

....

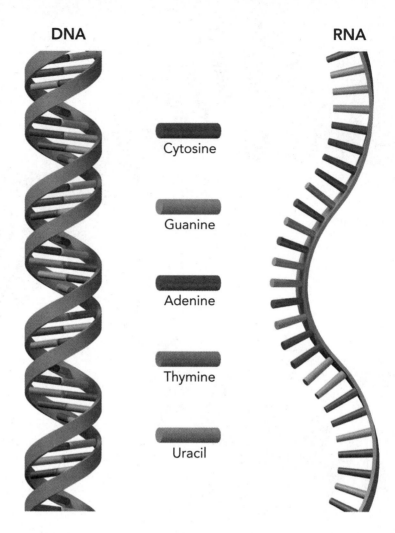

DNA

RNA

Cytosine

Guanine

Adenine

Thymine

Uracil

HANDS-ON LAB

Make a model of the process of protein synthesis.

Literacy Connection

Cite Textual Evidence Identify locations in both the diagram and the text that describe the similarities and differences between DNA and RNA.

Making Proteins

Proteins are made from building blocks called amino acids. There are only 20 amino acids in the human body, but your body can combine them in thousands of ways to make many different types of proteins needed to carry out cell processes. Inside the cell, amino acids link to form proteins through a process called **protein synthesis**. Once the protein is made, the cell will express the trait or perform a function.

RNA The process of protein synthesis starts in the nucleus, where the DNA contains the code for the protein. However, the actual assembly of the protein occurs at an organelle called the ribosome. Before a ribosome can assemble a protein, it needs to receive the blueprint to assemble the right protein from the nucleus.

The blueprint is transferred from the nucleus to the ribosome by a different nucleic acid called RNA (ribonucleic acid). Even though both RNA and DNA are nucleic acids, they have some differences. One difference is that RNA contains the sugar ribose instead of deoxyribose. **Figure 4** shows two other differences.

How RNA Is Used There are two main types of RNA involved in protein synthesis: messenger RNA and transfer RNA. **Messenger RNA** (mRNA) carries copies of instructions for the assembly of amino acids into proteins from DNA to ribosomes in the cytoplasm. **Transfer RNA** (tRNA), shown in **Figure 5**, carries amino acids to the ribosome during protein synthesis.

The order of the nitrogen bases on a gene determines the structure of the protein it makes. In the genetic code, a group of three nitrogen bases codes for one specific amino acid. For example, the three-base DNA sequence C-G-T (cytosine-guanine-thymine) always codes for the amino acid alanine. The order of the three-base code units determines the order in which amino acids are put together to form a protein. (**Figure 6**). See **Figure 7** for a summary of the entire process of protein synthesis.

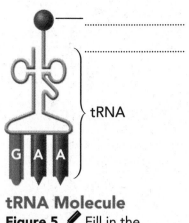

tRNA Molecule
Figure 5 ✏ Fill in the label to identify what tRNA molecules carry.

Knowing the Code

Figure 6 A codon is a sequence of three bases that codes for one amino acid. For the DNA sequence C-T-A, the complementary mRNA codon would be G-A-U. Since RNA does not have thymine, the RNA complement to adenine will always be uracil. Scientists use an mRNA codon table to determine which codons will code for each amino acid. The highlighted parts of the table show you how the codon G-A-U codes for aspartic acid, also known as aspartate.

mRNA Codon Table

First position		Second position				Third position
		U	C	A	G	
U		phenyl-alanine	serine	tyrosine	cysteine	U
						C
		leucine		stop	stop	A
				stop	tryptophan	G
C		leucine	proline	histidine	arginine	U
						C
				glutamine		A
						G
A		isoleucine	threonine	asparagine	serine	U
						C
		methionine/start		lysine	arginine	A
						G
G		valine	alanine	aspartic acid	glycine	U
						C
				glutamic acid		A
						G

1. **Synthesize Information** What is the mRNA sequence for the DNA sequence A-C-C?

....

2. **Use Tables** What amino acid is that mRNA sequence coding for?

....

3. **SEP Engage in Argument** Why would it be incorrect to say that the DNA sequence A-C-G codes for the amino acid threonine?

....

....

....

....

Protein Synthesis

Figure 7 Protein synthesis begins in the nucleus and ends at the ribosome.

INTERACTIVITY

Make a protein through protein synthesis.

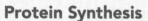

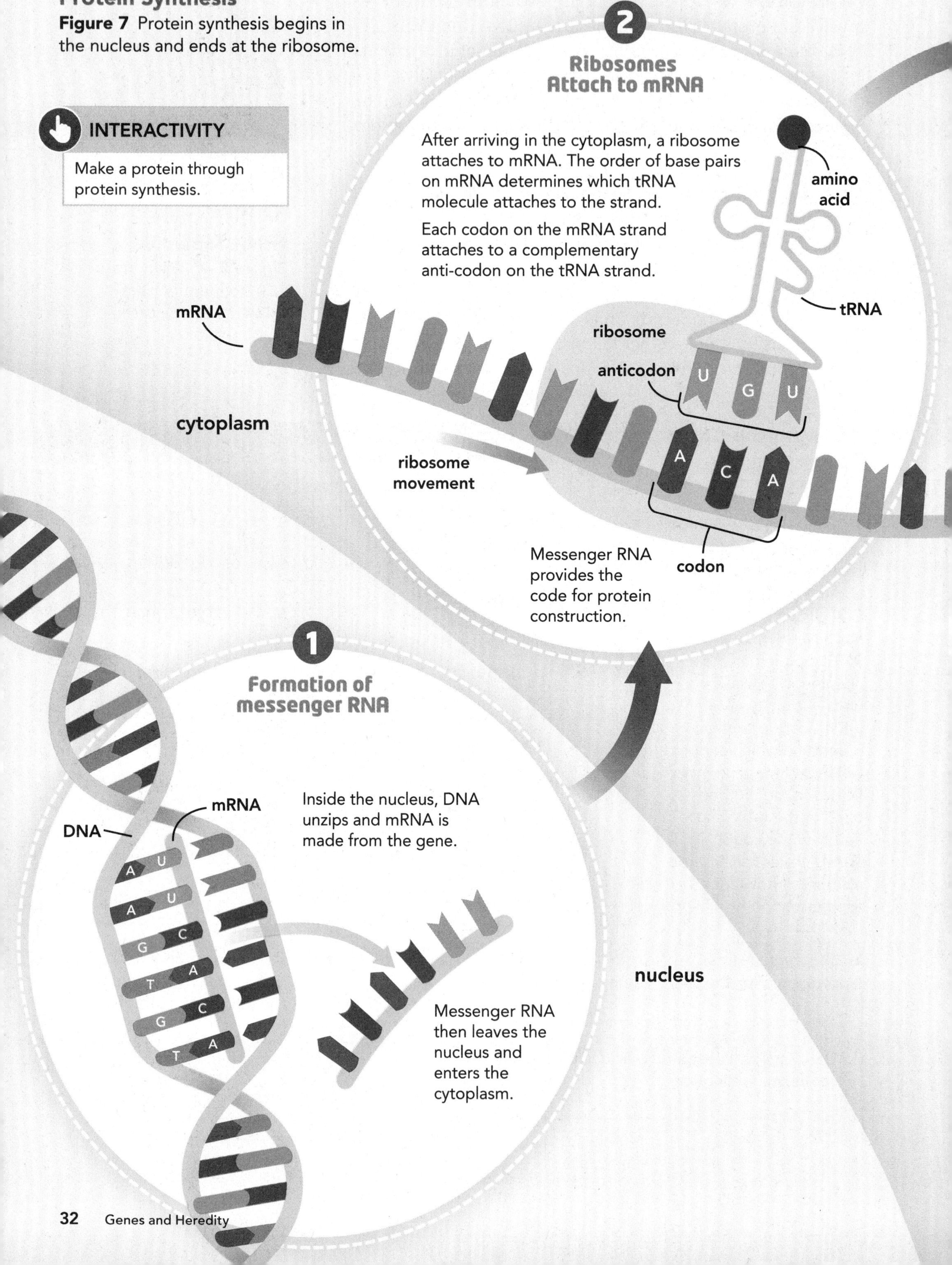

2
Ribosomes Attach to mRNA
After arriving in the cytoplasm, a ribosome attaches to mRNA. The order of base pairs on mRNA determines which tRNA molecule attaches to the strand.
Each codon on the mRNA strand attaches to a complementary anti-codon on the tRNA strand.
amino acid
tRNA
mRNA
ribosome
anticodon
U G U
cytoplasm
ribosome movement
A C A
Messenger RNA provides the code for protein construction.
codon
1
Formation of messenger RNA
Inside the nucleus, DNA unzips and mRNA is made from the gene.
mRNA
DNA
A U
A U
G C
T A
G C
T A
nucleus
Messenger RNA then leaves the nucleus and enters the cytoplasm.

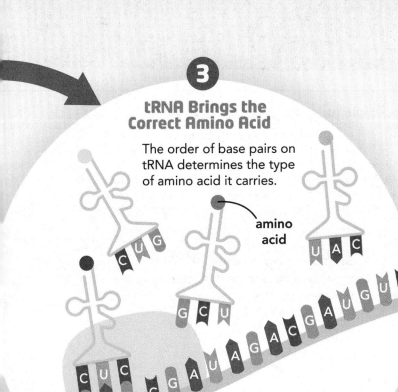

3 tRNA Brings the Correct Amino Acid

The order of base pairs on tRNA determines the type of amino acid it carries.

amino acid

As the ribosome moves along the mRNA strand, molecules of tRNA bring their attached amino acids.

4 Protein Chain Is Formed

protein chain

As tRNA anti-codons line up with mRNA codons, the amino acids bond at the ribosome and form a long protein chain.

Model It!

SEP Use Models ✏ Use the steps in **Figure 7** as a guide to fill in the missing molecules that drive each step of the process. Then complete the flowchart with the complementary nitrogen bases or amino acids (refer to codon table in **Figure 6**).

Step	Molecules
1 _____	T G T G A A
2 _____	☐ ☐ ☐ ☐ ☐ ☐
3 _____	☐ ☐ ☐ ☐ ☐ ☐
4 Protein	☐ ☐

☑LESSON 3 Check

MS-LS3-1

1. **CCC Identify Patterns** List the six nitrogen bases that would pair with the following sequence of bases in a strand of DNA: T C G A C A

....

2. **Explain Phenomena** Why does the cell complete DNA replication?

....

....

....

....

3. **Synthesize Information** What will happen to a protein when the DNA codes for a different amino acid?

....

....

4. **Support Your Explanation** Explain the importance of the sequence of nitrogen bases on a gene to heredity.

....

....

....

....

....

5. **CCC Analyze Structure and Function** DNA replication begins when the double helix untwists and breaks in half between the nitrogen bases. What are the next two steps in the process of DNA replication?

....

....

....

....

....

....

6. **SEP Construct Explanations** Explain the relationship of making proteins to inheritance of traits.

....

....

....

7. **SEP Develop Models** ✏ Sketch and label models of DNA and RNA that show the difference in their shapes, their sugars, and their nitrogen bases.

MS-LS3-1

REINVENTING DNA AS
Data Storage

▶ VIDEO
See how scientists use DNA to store digital information.

How much digital space

do you need for all your texts, emails, photos, and music? Digital information can take up lots of space.

Code	P	l	a	y
Binary data	01010000	01101100	01100001	01111001
DNA nucleotides	GCGAG	ATCGA	AGAGC	TGCTCT

The Challenge: To provide storage solutions for the data storage needs of everyone on Earth.

Phenomenon Some estimates state that the world has 40 trillion gigabytes (GB) of data. Forty trillion GB equals about 40 million petabytes (PB). Ten billion photos on social media sites use about 1.5 PB. So, if every star in our Milky Way galaxy were one byte of data, then we would need 5,000 Milky Ways, each with 200 billion stars, to amass one PB of data. How can we possibly store all of our data?

Nature may offer an answer: DNA. Our entire genetic code fits within the nucleus of a single cell. Scientists have figured out how to convert digital data (in 1s and 0s) into DNA's A-C-T-G code. Then they constructed synthetic DNA in a lab. So far, scientists have been able to encode and store images and videos within a single strand of DNA. If current cost constraints are overcome, DNA could be the next microchip. Someday, the data currently stored on computers in enormous buildings may fit in the palm of your hand!

Scientists can store documents and photos by converting digital code to DNA code and then making synthetic DNA. To retrieve a file, the DNA code gets converted back to digital code.

DESIGN CHALLENGE Can you design your own code to store information? Go to the Engineering Design Notebook to find out!

4 Trait Variations

Guiding Questions

- How do genes on sex chromosomes determine different traits?
- How do mutations affect protein synthesis and increase variation?
- How does the environment influence genetic traits?

Connections

Literacy Integrate with Visuals

Math Construct a Scatter Plot

MS-LS3-1, MS-LS4-4

HANDS-ON LAB

uInvestigate Observe physical traits found in a group of individuals.

Vocabulary

variation
sex chromosomes
autosomal chromosomes
mutation
sex-linked genes

Academic Vocabulary

sequence

Connect It!

🖊 **Circle a trait that distinguishes the male elephant seal from the female.**

Determine Differences What other differences do you notice between the male and female elephant seals?

....

....

CCC Structure and Function What traits allow the elephant seal to live in water? Explain your reasoning.

....

....

....

Diversity of Life

Organisms from the same species tend to have many similarities. The Northern elephant seals in **Figure 1**, however, show that very different traits can exist in two individuals. Some differences are visible traits, such as wrinkled skin or brown hair. Others are invisible, such as type I diabetes or sickle-cell anemia. Differences have the potential to be passed on from one generation to the next, and change the population.

The diversity of life on Earth relies in part on the variety of traits within a species. Any difference between individuals of the same species is a **variation**. Two friends with different eye color have a variation (green, brown) of the same trait (eye color). Variations may be due to DNA inherited from the parents, exposure to certain environmental factors, or a combination of both inheritance and environmental factors.

Variations can be helpful, harmful, or neutral. Consider a population of butterflies avoiding predators. Some have the same wing color pattern as a poisonous species. When this variation is passed from one generation to the next, the offspring are more likely to survive and reproduce. A harmful variation, on the other hand, threatens a population's survival. For example, low blood oxygen levels can be found in individuals with sickle-cell anemia. Neutral variations, such as different eye color, do not benefit or harm the population.

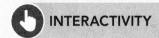
INTERACTIVITY

Identify traits found on a dog.

Northern Elephant Seals

Figure 1 Seals of the same species share most of the same DNA, yet there are differences in their appearance. This male (left) and female (right) relax near the ocean.

HANDS-ON LAB

⚗ **Investigate** Observe physical traits found in a group of individuals.

👆 INTERACTIVITY

Explore how some genetic disorders are carried on sex chromosomes.

Chromosomes and Variation

You received 23 chromosomes from your mother and 23 chromosomes from your father. The combination of genes found on these chromosomes codes for the proteins that determine your traits.

Types of Chromosomes There are two types of chromosomes found in every one of your cells. Of the 23 pairs of chromosomes, one pair is sex chromosomes, while the other 22 pairs are autosomal chromosomes. **Sex chromosomes** are the pair of chromosomes carrying genes that determine whether a person is biologically male or female.

The combination of sex chromosomes determines the sex of the offspring. A human female inherits one X chromosome from her mother and one X chromosome from her father. A male receives one X chromosome from his mother and one Y chromosome from his father. **Figure 2** compares the X and Y chromosomes.

The 22 pairs of chromosomes that are not sex chromosomes are **autosomal chromosomes**. You inherit half of your autosomal chromosomes from your mother and half from your father. All the pairs of autosomal chromosomes are homologous chromosomes. This means that the genes for a trait are located at the same place on each chromosome in the pair, even though the alleles may be different. Females also have homologous sex chromosomes, while males do not.

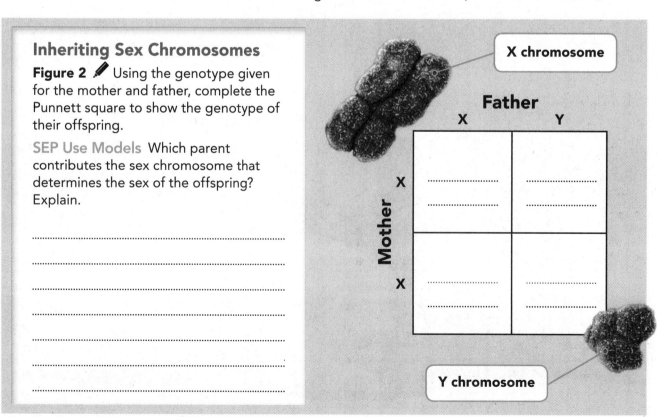

Inheriting Sex Chromosomes

Figure 2 🖉 Using the genotype given for the mother and father, complete the Punnett square to show the genotype of their offspring.

SEP Use Models Which parent contributes the sex chromosome that determines the sex of the offspring? Explain.

....

....

....

....

....

....

....

X chromosome

Father

X   Y

Mother   X

X

Y chromosome

Chromosomes Size Chromosomes contain DNA, and each section of DNA that codes for a protein is a gene. For every trait, there is a gene or group of genes that controls the trait by producing proteins through the process of protein synthesis. Because the number of genes found on each chromosome and the length of each gene varies, chromosomes come in different sizes. For example, the X chromosome is almost three times the size of the Y chromosome and contains close to 16 times as many genes. Thus, it codes for more proteins, and determines more traits.

✓READING CHECK **Cite Textual Evidence** Why does the X chromosome express more traits than the Y chromosome?

Math Toolbox

Chromosome and Gene Relationship

This data shows chromosome size as number of base pairs in the millions (Mbp) and estimated number of genes found on each one.

1. **Construct a Scatter Plot** ✏ Complete the scatter plot. Each dot represents the relationship between the total base pairs and the estimated number of genes for each chromosome.

Human Chromosome Size vs. Number of Genes

Estimated Number of Genes (y-axis: 0, 500, 1,000, 1,500, 2,000)
Millions of Base Pairs (Mbp) (x-axis: 0, 50, 100, 150, 200, 250)

2. **SEP Interpret Data** What relationship do you see between chromosome size and number of genes?

Chromosome	Mbp	Genes
1	248.96	2000
2	242.19	1300
3	198.3	1000
4	190.22	1000
5	181.54	900
6	170.81	1000
7	159.35	900
8	145.14	700
9	138.4	800
10	133.8	700
11	135.09	1300
12	133.28	1100
13	114.36	300
14	107.04	800
15	101.99	600
16	90.34	800
17	83.26	1200
18	80.37	200
19	58.62	1500
20	64.44	500
21	46.71	200
22	50.82	500
X	156.04	800
Y	57.23	50

Types of Mutations

An organism can develop traits due to changes in their genetic code. A **mutation** is any change in the DNA of a gene or chromosome. Mutations can be inherited from a parent or acquired during an organism's life. Inherited mutations occur when the parent passes on the mutation during reproduction. These mutations are present throughout the life of the organism, and are in every cell of the body. Acquired mutations occur at some point during an organism's lifetime. Acquired mutations can only be passed on from parent to offspring if the mutations occur in sex cells.

Academic Vocabulary

Explain a situation where you restated a sequence of events.

....

....

....

....

....

Genetic Mutations Many mutations are the result of small changes in the organism's DNA. Just one small change to a base pair is a mutation and may cause an incorrect protein to be made during protein synthesis. For example, the DNA **sequence** ATG is complimentary to the mRNA sequence UAC and codes for the amino acid tyrosine. If the second base were replaced, making the DNA sequence AGG (mRNA compliment UCC), it would code for the wrong amino acid, serine. As a result, the trait may be different from what was expressed before. Genetic mutations can occur between one base pair or several base pairs. **Figure 4** shows genetic mutations that can result when a base pair is deleted, added, or exchanged for different base pairs. **Figure 5** shows an example of a substitution mutation.

Literacy Connection

Integrate with Visuals ✏️
Find the three examples of mutation. Draw an arrow to show where a base pair was deleted. Circle where a base pair was added. Draw an X on the base pair that was substituted.

Genetic Mutations

Figure 4 The diagram shows three types of single base pair mutations.

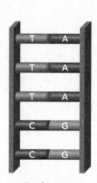
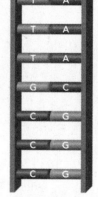

Original DNA sequence

Deletion: one base pair is removed.

Addition: one base pair is added.

Substitution: one base pair is switched for another.

Sex-Linked Mutations A mutation can occur on any chromosome. Some mutations occur on **sex-linked genes**, which are genes carried on a sex chromosome. Because the X chromosome has more genes than the Y chromosome, most sex-linked mutations occur on the X chromosome. In addition, many sex-linked mutations are recessive. Hemophilia is a recessive sex-linked mutation, where the individual's ability to clot blood is reduced. Males are more likely to exhibit hemophilia because they have only one X chromosome.

Model It

Mutations and Protein Construction

Figure 5 Sickle cell anemia results from a substitution mutation. The mutation alters the shape of red blood cells. Sickled cells can get stuck in blood vessels, blocking the flow of oxygenated blood cells.

SEP Develop Models Not all mutations result in new traits. Fill in the normal and mutated amino acid in the diagram below. Then, using the normal red blood cell DNA sequence, create a model that has one mutation, but will still make a normal protein. Refer to the mRNA Codon Table in Lesson 3, Genetic Coding and Protein Synthesis.

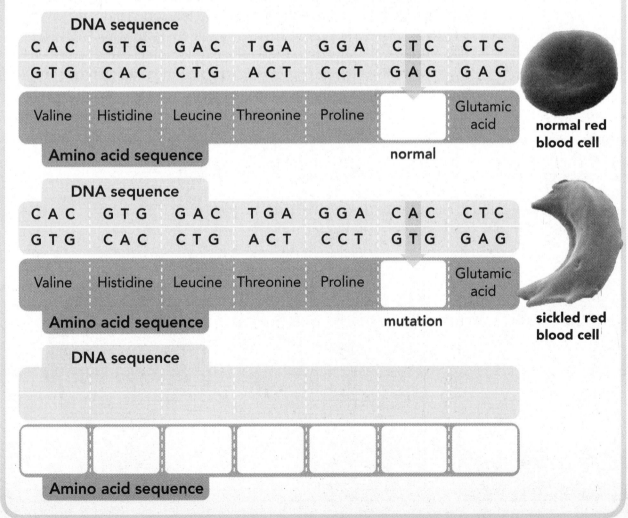

DNA sequence

| C A C | G T G | G A C | T G A | G G A | C T C | C T C |
| G T G | C A C | C T G | A C T | C C T | G A G | G A G |

| Valine | Histidine | Leucine | Threonine | Proline | | Glutamic acid |

Amino acid sequence   normal

normal red blood cell

DNA sequence

| C A C | G T G | G A C | T G A | G G A | C A C | C T C |
| G T G | C A C | C T G | A C T | C C T | G T G | G A G |

| Valine | Histidine | Leucine | Threonine | Proline | | Glutamic acid |

Amino acid sequence   mutation

sickled red blood cell

DNA sequence

Amino acid sequence

Environmental Factors

Interactions with our surroundings and the conditions in which we live have the potential to change the way genes are normally expressed. First, environment factors can change nucleotides, the building blocks of nucleic acids—DNA and RNA. Secondly, the chemicals found on DNA can be changed.

Organisms come in contact with harmful chemicals and radiation on a regular basis. These agents are called mutagens because they can damage DNA in such way that it causes mutations. Some mutagens naturally occur, while others are synthetic. For example, radiation in the form of ultraviolet (UV) or X-rays are naturally occurring mutagens. Synthetic mutagens can be found in pesticides, asbestos, and food additives.

Gene Expression Changes in the way genes are expressed may occur naturally or because of the environment. An example of natural change is when a caterpillar transitions to a butterfly. As the organism develops, the DNA does not change, but the genes are read and expressed differently.

The environment can change the way genes are expressed. Identical twins have the same DNA, but can acquire different traits when they grow up in different environments. Activities such as smoking and unhealthy eating habits can also alter the way genes are expressed, which changes a person's traits. **Figure 6** shows another way genes can be expressed differently.

Damage from Sun Exposure

Figure 6 ✏ UV radiation from the sun harms skin cells. UVA radiation penetrates into the deep layers of the skin. UVB radiation penetrates only the top layer of the skin. Draw arrows in the first diagram to show how deep UVA and UVB penetrate into the skin. Then, identify the radiation type—UVA or UVB—in the box next to the picture that shows a possible effect of the radation.

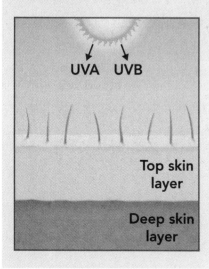

UVA   UVB

Top skin layer

Deep skin layer

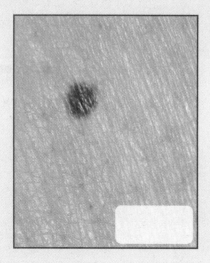

Mutation Effects Mutations may be harmful, helpful, or neutral. Helpful mutations are those that benefit the survival of the species and are often passed on to offspring. Harmful mutations do not benefit the species and often decrease the likelihood of survival. Neutral mutations are those that do not affect an organism's chance of survival.

Helpful Mutations Some mutations can help an organism survive in their environment. One example of a helpful mutation is camouflage. Possessing the ability to blend in with the environment, **Figure 7**, protects an organism from predators that may be looking for a meal. In humans, a mutation in a gene controlling fast-twitch muscles produces sprinters who are world class athletes.

Harmful Mutations Genetic disorders and cancer are both the result of harmful mutations. A genetic disorder is an abnormal condition that a person inherits through genes or chromosomes. Cystic fibrosis is a genetic disorder that causes the body to make thick mucus in the lungs and digestive system. The mucus builds up in the lungs and blocks air flow. Cancer is a disease in which some body cells grow and divide uncontrollably, damaging the parts of the body around them. Few cancers are inherited. Most cancers are caused by acquired mutations that occur from damage to genes during the life of an organism.

Neutral Mutations Not all mutations are helpful or harmful. Some mutations, such as human hair color, may be neutral and have no impact on the survival of an organism. There may also be mutations that still code for the same protein. Even though the DNA sequence has changed, the amino acid that is produced remains the same.

☑ READING CHECK **Distinguish Facts** In what ways can the environment impact the traits of an organism?

....

....

....

Mutations in Reproduction

Not all mutations are the result of small changes in an organism's DNA. Some mutations occur when chromosomes do not separate correctly during the formation of sex cells. When this happens, a sex cell can end up with too many or too few chromosomes. When a chromosomal mutation occurs, either additional proteins are created or fewer proteins are created.

During meiosis, sometimes DNA does not separate normally, instead staying together as the cell divides. This abnormal distribution of DNA is called a nondisjunction, shown in **Figure 8**.

Nondisjunction

Figure 8 DNA can separate abnormally during Meiosis I or Meiosis II.

1. **SEP Use Mathematics** Normal human sex cells have 23 chromosomes. Use the art to determine the number of chromosomes a sex cell may have if the nondisjuction occured during Meiosis I. Include all possible chromosome totals.

....

....

....

2. **SEP Use Models** What is the difference between the sex cells of a nondisjunction that occurred during meiosis I and the sex cells of a nondisjunction that occurred during meiosis II?

....

....

....

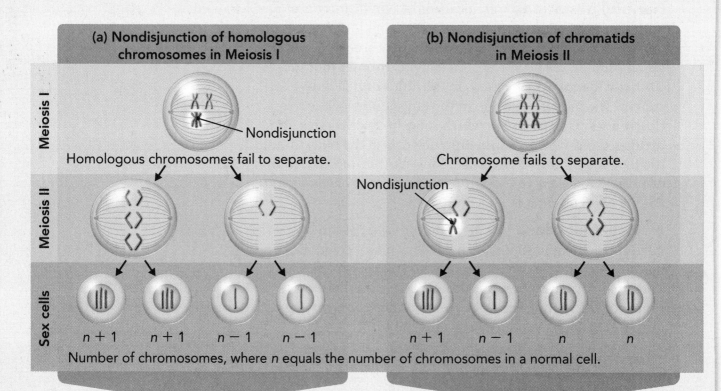

(a) Nondisjunction of homologous chromosomes in Meiosis I

Meiosis I

Nondisjunction

Homologous chromosomes fail to separate.

Meiosis II

Sex cells

$n + 1$ $n + 1$ $n - 1$ $n - 1$

(b) Nondisjunction of chromatids in Meiosis II

Chromosome fails to separate.

Nondisjunction

$n + 1$ $n - 1$ n n

Number of chromosomes, where n equals the number of chromosomes in a normal cell.

Resulting sex cells either have additional DNA or not enough DNA.

Resulting sex cells could have one additional chromosome, one less chromosome, or the normal number of chromosomes.

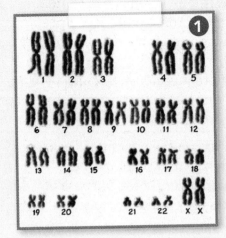

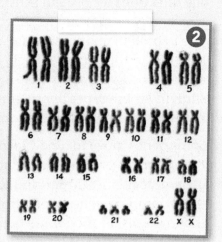

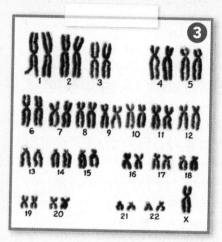

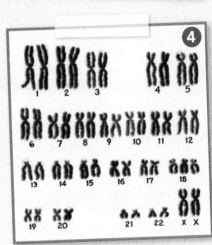

Comparing Karyotypes

Figure 9 🖊 Karyotype 1 shows what chromosomes would look like without a nondisjunction. Circle the chromosomes in the second, third, and forth karyotypes that indicate a nondisjunction occurred.

1. **SEP Use Models** What is the sex of the individual found represented in the first karyotpe?

   ....

2. **Apply Concepts** How would a scientist name the disorder represented by the third karyotype?

   ....

Karyotypes Sometimes, doctors suspect that an individual has a genetic disorder based on observable traits. To accurately determine if an individual has a chromosomal mutation, a scientist will create a karotype **(Figure 9),** which is a picture of all the chromosomes in a person's cell and then arrange the chromosomes by size and matching chromosome patterns. Homologous chromosomes are paired to provide a quick overview. The karyotypes on this page compare a normal individual and three individuals with genetic disorders. If there is an additional chromosome, the grouping is called a trisomy (*tri-* means "three" and *somy*, from Greek *soma* for *body*, indicates a chromosome). If one chromosome is missing, it is a monosomy (*mono-* means "one"). In addition, scientists include the homologous number and often assign a common name to the disorder. For example, trisomy 18 is Edward's Syndrome, while trisomy 21 is Down's Syndrome.

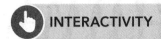
Protein Changes Amino acids are the building blocks of proteins, which can be considered the architects of cell function. A change in the amino acid sequence can alter the directions for protein synthesis. The result is a mutation, which may or may not be detectable. Some mutations arise due to protein changes caused when genes move to a different location on the genome. There are also a few species that can alter their RNA to synthesize different proteins. Scientists are studying these types of protein changes to understand any benefits they might bring to an organism.

Some genes move to a new location on the genome. When this occurs, it produces the protein at that point on the genome. Scientists are trying to understand the purpose of these 'jumping genes'. Sometimes they jump to a location that disrupts a functioning gene. When this occurs, the gene is not able to express itself, which can cause traits to change. Scientists speculate that jumping genes may cause a species to change.

Scientists recently discovered that some species of octopus and squid, such as the one shown in **Figure 10**, are able to change their RNA. Since RNA is needed for the construction of proteins, they are able make different proteins. Scientists believe that these organisms are able to create specific proteins in response to a changing environment.

Changing RNA

Figure 10 Organisms, like this squid, are able to change their RNA, thus changing the proteins that are constructed.

Synthesize Information Why is it beneficial for scientists to understand how other organisms are able to edit their RNA?

....

....

....

....

☑ READING CHECK **Determine Central Ideas** When a gene jumps, what might happen to the organism's traits?

....

....

....

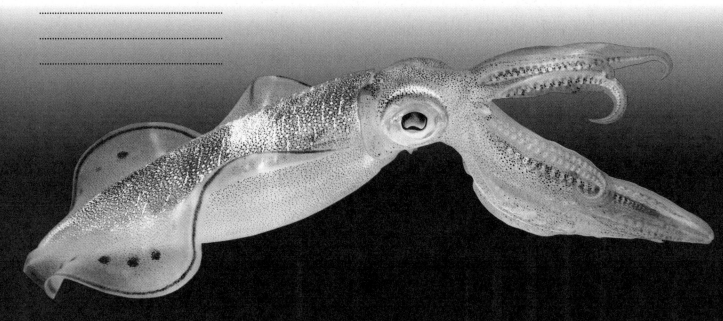

MS-LS3-1, MS-LS4-4

1. **Communicate** How many and what types of chromosomes are found in every one of your cells?

....

....

2. **Determine Differences** How are inherited mutations different from acquired mutations?

....

....

....

....

3. **SEP Construct Explanations** How is an organism's ability to produce offspring affected by changes to a chromosome?

....

....

....

....

....

....

4. **Evaluate Claims** A student states that only a male human offspring can express a recessive sex-linked X chromosome mutation. Is this statement accurate? Explain.

....

....

....

....

....

5. **SEP Develop Models** 🖊 Red-green color blindness is a sex-linked recessive condition. Its gene is located on the X chromosome. Most people with red-green color blindness cannot see the difference in shades of red and green. Suppose a heterozygous female ($X^N X^n$) has offspring with a male who is color blind ($X^n Y$). Draw a Punnett square. Label each offspring as applicable: normal vision, carrier, or color blind. (X^N indicates normal vision; X^n indicates color blindness.)

Quest CHECK-IN

In this lesson, you learned that organisms can inherit traits, acquire traits, and some organisms can change their traits.

Support Your Explanation Why are the desired traits you selected for your fruit not always a guarantee that your fruit will have those traits? Provide support.

....

....

....

....

....

....

HANDS-ON LAB

All in the Numbers

Do the hands-on lab to complete the investigation and discover how experimental results may vary from probability. You will make observations and test the crossing of traits.

5 Genetic Technologies

Guiding Questions

- How do humans use artificial selection to produce organisms with desired traits?
- How do scientists engineer new genes?
- How can genetic information be used?

Connection

Literacy Corroborate

MS-LS4-5

HANDS-ON LAB

uInvestigate Extract DNA from a strawberry.

Vocabulary

artificial
  selection
genetic
  engineering
gene therapy
clone
genome

Academic Vocabulary

manipulation

Connect It !

🖊 **Dogs come in many different shapes, sizes, and colors. Which of the ones shown here would you prefer as a pet? Circle your choice.**

Apply Concepts Many purebred dogs have problems later in life, such as joint or eye diseases. Why are purebred dogs more likely to develop problems later in life?

....

....

SEP Design Solutions What can be done to decrease the likelihood of these problems appearing?

....

....

Artificial Selection

When consumers make choices, they are often attracted to products with the highest quality. We want the healthiest and best-tasting fruits and vegetables. We want the right amount of fat and flavor in our meats. We even want the best traits in our pets, such as the dogs you see in **Figure 1**. These high-quality products do not appear only in nature. Scientists and breeders have influenced the traits that other organisms inherit through the process of selective breeding.

Selective Breeding In the natural world, individuals with beneficial traits are more likely to survive and successfully reproduce than individuals without those traits. This is called natural selection. **Artificial selection** is also known as selective breeding. It occurs when humans breed only those organisms with desired traits to produce the next generation. It's important to note that desired traits are not necessarily the traits that benefit the organism's chances for survival. Instead, they are traits that humans desire.

Dogs, cats, and livestock animals have all been selectively bred. Cows, chickens, and pigs have been bred to be larger so that they produce more milk or meat. Breeding and caring for farm animals that have certain genetic traits that humans desire is called animal husbandry. The many different breeds of dogs shown in **Figure 1** have also been bred over time for very specific functions.

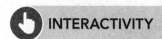

INTERACTIVITY

Consider how artificial selection affects the traits of dogs.

Literacy Connection

Corroborate Find statements in the text that support the claim that artificial selection is not a natural process and does not necessarily help the organism's survival.

Purebred Dogs

Figure 1 Each type of purebred dog shown here is the result of selective breeding over the course of many generations.

Genetic Engineering

With the discovery of DNA and its relationship to genes, scientists have developed more methods to produce desired traits. Through a process called **genetic engineering**, modern geneticists can transfer a gene from the DNA of one organism into another. Genetic engineering is used to give organisms genes they could not acquire through breeding.

Glowing Fish

Figure 2 Genetic engineering made glowing fish possible.

Scientists use genetic engineering techniques to insert specific desired genes into animals. By **manipulating** a gene, scientists have created a fish that glows when under a black light **(Figure 2)**. A jellyfish gene for fluorescence was inserted into a fertilized fish egg to produce the glowing fish. Scientists are hoping that further research on this gene will lead to a method that helps track toxic chemicals in the body.

Academic Vocabulary

Explain the difference between manipulating a tool and manipulating another person.

....

....

....

....

....

....

....

Genetic engineering is also used to synthesize materials. A protein called insulin helps control blood-sugar levels after eating. People who have diabetes cannot effectively control their blood-sugar levels, and many must take insulin injections. Prior to 1980, some diabetics were injecting themselves with insulin from other animals without getting the desired results. To help diabetics, scientists genetically engineered bacteria to produce the first human protein — insulin. The process they used, and still use today, is shown in **Figure 3**. Furthermore, bacteria can reproduce quickly, so large amounts of human insulin are produced in a short time.

Plan It

Synthesize a New Trait

✎ Create a trait that has never been seen before in an animal. Identify a trait you would like an animal to have. Then, sketch the animal and describe a process by which you could achieve your desired result.

....

....

....

....

....

....

....

Bacteria Make Human Insulin

Figure 3 🖉 Bacteria can be used to produce insulin in humans. Complete the diagram by showing the process for Step 5.

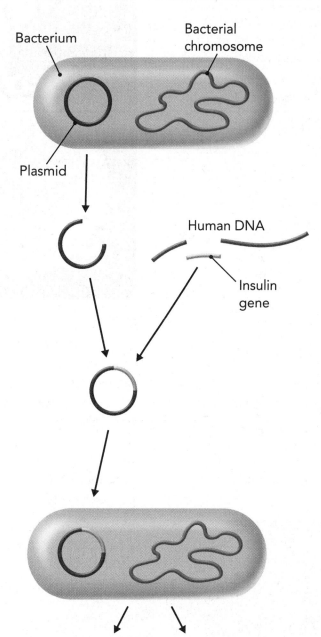

❶ Small rings of DNA, or plasmids, are found in some bacteria cells.

❷ Scientists remove the plasmid and cut it open with an enzyme. They then insert an insulin gene that has been removed from human DNA.

❸ The human insulin gene attaches to the open ends of the plasmid to form a closed ring.

❹ Some bacteria cells take up the plasmids that have the insulin gene.

❺ When the cells reproduce, the new cells contain copies of the "engineered" plasmid. The foreign gene directs the cells to produce human insulin.

51

T-cell Destroys Cancer Cell

Figure 4 T-cells are a type of white blood cell that help to fight disease in your body. Scientists have genetically engineered a T-cell that can attack and destroy up to 1,000 cancer cells.

Predict How might doctors use this new T-cell?

....

....

....

....

....

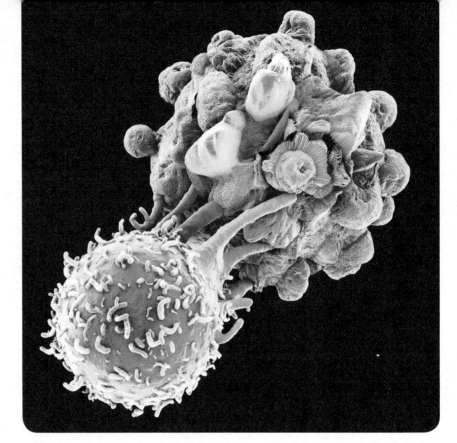

Sickle-cell Disease

Figure 5 Sickle-shaped red blood cells cannot carry as much oxygen as normal cells and can also clog blood vessels.

Gene Therapy in Humans Genetic diseases are caused by mutations, or changes in the DNA code. Some mutated genes pass from parent to child; others occur spontaneously. Soon, it may be possible to use genetic engineering to correct some genetic disorders in humans. This process, called **gene therapy**, involves changing a gene to treat a medical disease or disorder. A normal working gene replaces an absent or faulty gene. One promising therapy involves genetically engineering immune-system cells and injecting them into a person's body.

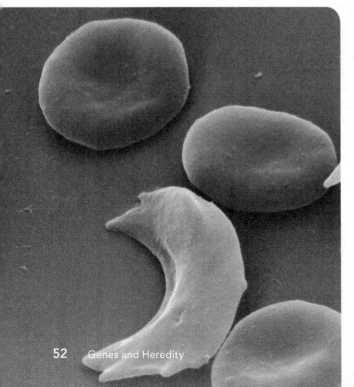

Millions of people worldwide suffer from sickle cell disease. This painful genetic disorder is caused by a singe mutation that affects hemoglobin, a protein in red blood cells. Hemoglobin carries oxygen. The mutation causes the blood cells to be shaped like a sickle, or crescent, as shown in **Figure 5.**

CRISPR is a gene-editing tool that can help people with sickle cell disease. CRISPR uses a "guide RNA" and an enzyme to cut out the DNA sequence causing the dangerous mutation. The "guide RNA" takes the enzyme to the DNA sequence with the sickle cell mutation, and the enzyme then removes that sequence. Then another tool pastes a copy of the normal sequence into the DNA.

Cloning Organisms

A **clone** is an organism that has the same genes as the organism from which it was produced. The process of cloning involves removing an unfertilized egg and replacing its nucleus with the nucleus of a body cell from the same species. Because this body cell has a full set of chromosomes, the offspring will have the same DNA as the individual that donated the body cell. The egg is then implanted into a female so it can develop. If the process is successful, the clone is born.

Cloning is used to develop many of the foods we eat. Many plants are cloned simply by taking a small piece of the original and putting it in suitable conditions to grow. For example, the Cavendish banana (see **Figure 6**) is the most common banana for eating. All these bananas are clones of the original plant. Cloning helps to produce crops of consistent quality. But a population with little genetic diversity has drawbacks.

☑ **READING CHECK** **Summarize Text** List the steps to creating a clone.

....

....

....

....

▶ **VIDEO**

Learn how selective breeding and cloning can lead to populations with desired traits.

Cloned Bananas

Figure 6 A fungus that causes bananas to rot is spreading across the globe. The Cavendish banana is particularly vulnerable.

SEP Construct Explanations Why is a disease more damaging to cloned crops?

....

....

....

....

....

Genetic Cousins

Figure 7 Humans and modern-day chimpanzees share about 99 percent of their DNA.

Infer How does knowing we are close genetically to chimpanzees help humans?

....

....

....

....

....

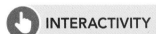

INTERACTIVITY

Gather fingerprints and identify who committed a crime.

Practical Uses for DNA

Due to new technologies, geneticists now study and use genes in ways that weren't possible before. Modern geneticists can now determine the exact sequence of nitrogen bases in an organism's DNA. This process is called DNA sequencing.

Sequencing the Human Genome Breaking a code with six billion letters may seem like an impossible task to undertake. But scientists working on the Human Genome Project did just that. The complete set of genetic information that an organism carries in its DNA is called a **genome**. The main goal of the Human Genome Project was to identify the DNA sequence of the entire human genome. Since sequencing the human genome, scientists now research the functions of tens of thousands of human genes. Some of these genes also allow scientists to better understand certain diseases.

Our genome can also help us understand how humans evolved on Earth. All life on Earth evolved from simple, single-celled organisms that lived billions of years ago, and we still have evidence of this in our DNA. For example, there are some genes that exist in the cells of almost every organism on Earth, which suggests we all evolved from a common ancestor. Some organisms share a closer relationship than others. By comparing genomes of organisms, scientists continue to piece together a history of how life on Earth evolved.

DNA Technologies

DNA Technologies Before the Human Genome Project, scientists such as Gregor Mendel used experimentation to understand heredity. Since the project's completion in 2003, the use of technologies to understand heredity and how DNA guides life processes has increased greatly. For example, DNA technologies help diagnose genetic diseases.

Genetic disorders typically result from one or more changed genes, called mutations. Medical specialists can carry out a DNA screening to detect the presence of a mutation. To complete a DNA screen, samples of DNA are analyzed for the presence of one or more mutated genes. This information is then used to help those individuals whose DNA includes mutated genes.

DNA comparisons determine how closely related you are to another person. To do this, DNA from a person's cell is broken down into small pieces, or fragments. These fragments are put into a machine that separates them by size. When this happens, a pattern is produced creating a DNA fingerprint, like the one shown in **Figure 8**. Similarities between patterns determine who contributed the DNA. Genetic fingerprints can be used to tie a person to a crime scene, prevent the wrong person from going to jail, identify remains, or identify the father of a child.

INTERACTIVITY

Consider using technology to solve the world's food problem.

DNA Fingerprint

Figure 8 🖊 Circle the suspect that left his or her DNA at the crime scene.

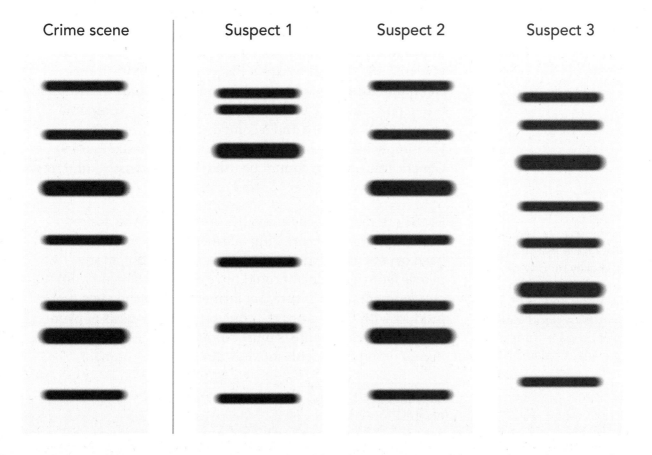

Crime scene   Suspect 1   Suspect 2   Suspect 3

Using Genetic Information

Figure 9 Some people fear that medical insurance companies will not cover their medical expenses if they have been genetically tested and results show a genetic disorder.

Evaluate Reasoning Why is this a fear of many people? What can we do to protect our privacy?

....
....
....
....
....
....
....
....
....

Write About It

Organ transplants save lives. Scientists have learned how to genetically modify pigs in order to grow human organs for transplant. Do you think it's a good idea to transplant organs from pigs into humans? Explain.

Controversies of DNA Use As genetic research advances, some people are concerned about how genetic information will be used or altered. Some people are concerned about the use of genetically modified organisms (GMOs) in our food supply. Others worry about who can access their DNA information, and how this information will be used.

Your genetic information is a big part of your identity, and many people want to keep it as private as possible. The Genetic Information Nondiscrimination Act (GINA) was signed into law in 2008. This act makes it illegal for health insurance companies and employers to discriminate against individuals based on genetic information. Health insurance companies cannot deny you care and a company cannot refuse to hire you simply because of the results of a genetic test (**Figure 9**). Genetic information cannot be used without consent, and must be used in a way that is fair and just.

GMOs are made by changing the original DNA so desired traits are expressed. Growing our food from seeds that have been genetically modified is highly controversial. Many people fear the impact it could have on human health and the environment in the future. Yet farmers are able to yield more product with GMO crops that are not eaten by pests or overcome by weeds. Scientists must balance sustaining a growing human population with safeguarding the environment.

✓ READING CHECK **Corroborate** What are the pros and cons of GMO foods?

....
....

MS-LS4-5

1. **Identify** Shortly after World War II, chickens were bred to grow much more quickly and to produce much more meat. What is this an example of?

....

2. **Compare and Contrast** What are some positive and negative ways that genetic information may be used?

....

....

....

3. **CCC Cause and Effect** Some genetically engineered organisms can mate with wild species. Farmed fish are often genetically modified. What can happen to the wild offspring of their species if mating occurs?

....

....

....

4. **SEP Construct Explanations** Gorillas and humans evolved from a common ancestor. Geneticists found that they may be more closely related than previously thought. How can DNA sequencing of the gorilla and human genomes determine this?

....

....

....

....

5. **SEP Evaluate Information** A classmate states that animals that result from artificial selection are "lucky," since they have better traits than naturally bred animals. Given your study of this topic, do you agree? Explain.

....

....

....

....

6. **CCC Relate Structure and Function** How can changes to the structure of DNA lead to the development of new traits in a species?

....

....

....

....

....

....

....

....

....

....

7. **SEP Design Solutions** The procedure used to make insulin in bacteria can also be used to synthesize other biological materials. Think of a chemical or material inside the human body that could be synthesized within bacteria. What would be the potential benefits of this process? What would be the potential drawbacks?

....

....

....

....

....

....

....

....

....

....

....

....

① Patterns of Inheritance

MS-LS3-2

1. Genes are carried from parents to offspring on structures called
   A. alleles.
   B. chromosomes.
   C. phenotypes.
   D. genotypes.

2. Which of the following represents a heterozygous genotype?
   A. GG
   B. gg
   C. Gg
   D. none of the above

3. An organism's phenotype is the way its
   .... is expressed.

4. **SEP Use a Model** ✏ Fill in the Punnett Square to show a cross between two guinea pigs who are heterozygous for coat color. *B* is for black coat color and *b* is for white coat color.

5. **Interpret Tables** What is the probability that an offspring from the cross in Question 9 has the genotype *bb*?

   ....

② Chromosomes and Inheritance

MS-LS3-2

6. Chromosomes are long, thread-like structures of
   A. cells.
   B. proteins.
   C. genes.
   D. DNA.

7. Which process results in the formation of sex cells?
   A. crossing over
   B. meiosis
   C. separation
   D. transfer

8. Geneticists use a ....
   to map the inheritance of particular traits.

9. **Apply Concepts** Each body cell in the American black bear has 74 chromosomes. How many chromosomes are in the black bear's sex cells? Explain your answer.

   ....

   ....

   ....

10. **SEP Construct Explanations** In sexual reproduction, if each chromosome in a pair has the same genes, how is genetic variety possible?

    ....

    ....

    ....

    ....

    ....

    ....

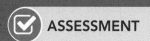

3 Genetic Coding and Protein Synthesis

MS-LS3-1

11. A gene is a section of DNA within a chromosome that codes for a(n)
   A. amino acid.
   B. specific protein.
   C. ribosome.
   D. double helix.

12. Proteins are long-chain molecules made of
   A. nitrogen bases.
   B. chromosomes.
   C. amino acids.
   D. organisms.

13. Draw Conclusions How does the pairing of nitrogen bases in a DNA molecule make sure that a replicated strand is exactly the same as the original strand?

....

....

....

....

....

4 Trait Variations

MS-LS3-1, MS-LS4-4

14. A female human has
   A. one X chromosome.
   B. two X chromosomes.
   C. one Y chromosome.
   D. two Y chromosomes.

15. SEP Engage in Argument A friend says that all genetic mutations are harmful. Do you agree or disagree with this statement? Why?

....

....

....

5 Genetic Technologies

MS-LS4-5

16. Genetic diseases are caused by
   A. X chromosomes.
   B. modified cells.
   C. plasmids.
   D. mutations.

17. Which of the following is the best example of a possible future technology that could be used to eliminate sickle cell disease in humans?
   A. a genetically engineered virus which can eliminate sickle-shaped cells in human blood
   B. genetic screening which matches sickle cell carriers to people with AA genotypes
   C. the ability to replace all S alleles in human red blood cells
   D. the ability to replace all S alleles in fertilized eggs

18. Scientists created a new variety of rice. They modified a common strain of rice by inserting the carotene gene from carrots. The addition of this gene resulted in a rice enriched with vitamin-A, a crucial vitamin for humans. What technology does this example represent?
   A. meiosis
   B. genetic engineering
   C. artificial selection
   D. cloning

19. Support Your Explanation The technology of genetic engineering holds great promise, yet it frightens some people. What are the advantages and disadvantages of genetic engineering?

....

....

....

....

....

MS-LS3-1, MS-LS4-4,
MS-LS4-5

Evidence-Based Assessment

Scientists have figured out a way to insert the genes of one organism into another. A genetically modified organism, GMO, expresses desired traits that prove to be beneficial to many farmers. Reliance on GMO crops has been increasing in the United States for many years.

The graph shows three genetically modified crops—corn, soybeans, and cotton. In each crop, the DNA has been engineered for a desired trait. New DNA sequences that code for specific proteins are inserted into a crop's DNA.

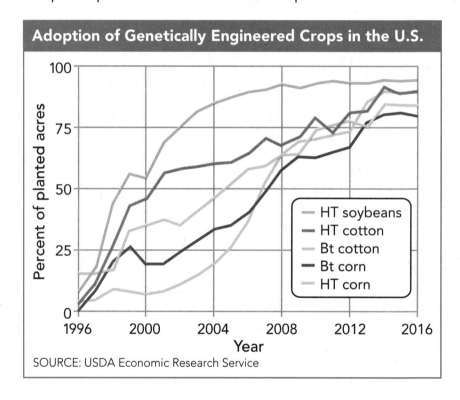

Adoption of Genetically Engineered Crops in the U.S.

- HT soybeans
- HT cotton
- Bt cotton
- Bt corn
- HT corn

SOURCE: USDA Economic Research Service

For example, some crops have been engineerd to resist droughts. The gene for drought resistance is spliced from the DNA of a desert-dwelling species and then inserted into the crop species. The resistance-to-drought trait will be expressed when these genetically engineered crop plants reproduce. Another desirable trait that has been produced through genetic engineering is improved herbicide tolerance (HT). This trait protects the GMO crop when herbicides are sprayed on the fields to kill weeds. In the case of the Bt crops, the desired gene comes from the *Bacillus thuringiensis* bacterium. The gene produces a protein that destroys the corn borer larvae. Farmers can grow Bt crops instead of spraying insecticides that could also kill helpful insects, such as bees.

1. **SEP Analyze Data** Which genetically engineered crop has shown the greatest increase in usage from 2006 to 2016?
   A. HT Corn
   B. Bt Corn
   C. HT Cotton
   D. HT Soybeans

2. **CCC Patterns** What patterns do you observe in the line graphs for the crops that are herbicide tolerant, HT? Support your claim.

   ....
   ....
   ....
   ....
   ....
   ....
   ....
   ....
   ....
   ....
   ....

3. **Connect to the Environment** What would be an advantage and a disadvantage to increased reliance on genetically engineered crops?

   ....
   ....
   ....
   ....
   ....
   ....
   ....
   ....
   ....
   ....

4. **SEP Construct Arguments** Based on the data, will genetically engineered crops continue to be used in the future? Explain.

   ....
   ....
   ....
   ....
   ....
   ....
   ....
   ....
   ....
   ....
   ....

Quest FINDINGS

Complete the Quest!

Phenomenon Create a brochure for prospective growers of your new fruit. Convince readers that your fruit will be a delicious success!

SEP Construct Arguments How will you know which traits are most beneficial to the general public so you can use them to create your fruit?

....
....
....
....

INTERACTIVITY

Reflect on Funky Fruits

MS-LS3-2

Make the Right Call!

How can you design and use a **model** to make **predictions** about the possible results of **genetic crosses**?

Background

Phenomenon Suppose your neighbors tell you that their cat is going to have kittens. They can't stop talking about what color they think the kittens will be and whether their hair will be long or short. Using the suggested materials and your knowledge of genetic crosses, how can you make a model to show your neighbors the probabilities of the possible color and hair length combinations for the kittens?

Your neighbors got both the mother and father cat from a respected breeder. The index card shows background information about the two cats.

Max, male cat, short hair, homozygous black hair.

Willa, female cat, heterozygous short hair, heterozygous black hair.

Materials

(per group)

- 4 small paper bags
- 12 red marbles
- 12 blue marbles
- 12 green marbles
- 12 yellow marbles
- marking pen

Design Your Investigation

Demonstrate Go online for a downloadable worksheet of this lab.

1. In the space below, use Punnett squares to determine the possible outcomes from a cross between the male and female cats. **TIP: First identify each parent's alleles, noting that all of them are known.**

Homozygous — parent or offspring has either two dominant or two recessive alleles.

Heterozygous — parent or offspring has one of each allele (one dominant and one recessive)

Dominant Trait	Recessive Trait
Short Hair	Long Hair
Black Hair	Brown Hair

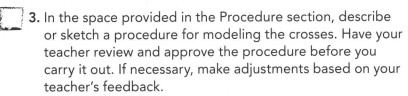

2. Design a way to model these crosses using the marbles and bags. The bags should contain the alleles of the male and female parent cats—two bags for each parent (one bag for hair color, the other bag for hair length). **TIP: Use four marbles for each allele in each cat.**

3. In the space provided in the Procedure section, describe or sketch a procedure for modeling the crosses. Have your teacher review and approve the procedure before you carry it out. If necessary, make adjustments based on your teacher's feedback.

4. Use your model. Record your observations in the data tables.

Procedure

....
....
....
....
....
....
....
....
....

Observations

Data Table 1 Hair Length			
Trial Cross	Allele from Bag 1 (Max)	Allele from Bag 2 (Willa)	Offspring's Alleles
1			
2			
3			
4			
5			
6			
7			
8			
9			
10			
11			
12			

Data Table 2 Hair Color			
Trial Cross	Allele from Bag 3 (Max)	Allele from Bag 4 (Willa)	Offspring's Alleles
1			
2			
3			
4			
5			
6			
7			
8			
9			
10			
11			
12			

Analyze and Interpret Data

1. **SEP Develop a Model** How did you use the materials? What did the different parts of the model represent?

   ....

   ....

   ....

2. **SEP Analyze Data** Refer to your Punnett squares. What percentages of black kittens (BB or Bb) and brown kittens (bb) did you predict? What percentages of shorthair kittens (SS or Ss) and longhair (ss) kittens did you predict?

   ....

   ....

   ....

3. **SEP Use a Model to Evaluate** Refer to your data table. Did the percentages of offspring with a given genotype match the percentages that you obtained by completing the Punnett squares? Explain.

   ....

   ....

   ....

   ....

4. **Compare Data** How did using a Punnett square differ from using your model? Which did you prefer?

   ....

   ....

   ....

   ....

   ....

5. **Form an Opinion** Was your model effective at showing the neighbors all of the possible combinations of hair color and length to expect in their kittens? Explain.

   ....

   ....

   ....

   ....

TOPIC 2

Natural Selection and Change Over Time

NGSS PERFORMANCE EXPECTATIONS

MS-LS4-1 Analyze and interpret data for patterns in the fossil record that document the existence, diversity, extinction, and change of life forms throughout the history of life on Earth under the assumption that natural laws operate today as in the past.

MS-LS4-2 Apply scientific ideas to construct an explanation for the anatomical similarities and differences among modern organisms and between modern and fossil organisms to infer evolutionary relationships.

MS-LS4-3 Analyze displays of pictorial data to compare patterns of similarities in the embryological development across multiple species to identify relationships not evident in the fully formed anatomy.

MS-LS4-4 Construct an explanation based on evidence that describes how genetic variations of traits in a population increase some individuals' probability of surviving and reproducing in a specific environment.

MS-LS4-5 Gather and synthesize information about the technologies that have changed the way humans influence the inheritance of desired traits in organisms.

MS-LS4-6 Use mathematical representations to support explanations of how natural selection may lead to increases and decreases of specific traits in populations over time.

Has this dragonfly changed from its fossilized ancestor?

GO ONLINE
to access your digital course

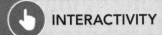

▶ VIDEO

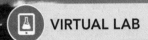

👆 INTERACTIVITY

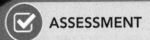

📱 VIRTUAL LAB

☑ ASSESSMENT

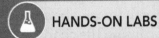

📖 eTEXT

⚗ HANDS-ON LABS

HANDS-ON LAB

uConnect Analyze evidence that whales may have walked on land.

The Essential Question — How do characteristics change over time?

CCC Structure and Function At first glance, this modern-day dragonfly and its fossilized ancestor probably don't look very different. Both seem to have long, slender bodies, two sets of wings, and large eyes. Would it surprise you to know that the dragonfly ancestor, *Meganeura*, lived about 300 million years ago and had a wingspan of 75 cm? It's the largest known flying insect! In comparison, the largest modern dragonfly has a wingspan of only 16 cm. Think about why we don't see such large insects anymore. List your ideas below.

....

....

....

Quest KICKOFF

Why is the migration pattern changing for some European bird populations?

NBC LEARN ▶ VIDEO

After watching the Quest Kickoff video about migrating golden eagles, list some of the factors that might affect the birds' migration patterns and routes.

....

....

....

....

....

....

....

Phenomenon To understand how bird populations change over time in response to environmental conditions, ornithologists (scientists who study birds) analyze long-term data. In this problem-based Quest activity, you will investigate factors that may be influencing changes in two populations of European blackcaps. By applying what you learn from each lesson, digital activity, and hands-on lab, you will determine what is causing the changes to the bird populations. Then in the Findings activity, you will prepare a multimedia report to communicate what you have learned and to explain the changes in the blackcap populations.

 INTERACTIVITY

A Migration Puzzle

MS-LS4-1 Analyze and interpret data for patterns in the fossil record that document the existence, diversity, extinction, and change of life forms throughout the history of life on Earth under the assumption that natural laws operate today as in the past.

MS-LS4-2 Apply scientific ideas to construct an explanation for the anatomical similarities and differences among modern organisms and between modern and fossil organisms to infer evolutionary relationships.

MS-LS4-3 Analyze displays of pictorial data to compare patterns of similarities in the embryological development across multiple species to identify relationships not evident in the fully formed anatomy.

MS-LS4-4 Construct an explanation based on evidence that describes how genetic variations of traits in a population increase some individuals' probability of surviving and reproducing in a specific environment.

Quest CHECK-IN

IN LESSON 1
What differences exist between the UK and Spanish blackcaps? Determine evidence for variations in the European blackcap population.

 INTERACTIVITY

Meet the Blackcaps

IN LESSON 2
What are the roles of genes and mutations in natural selection? Think about how you can include these factors in your report.

Quest CHECK-IN

IN LESSON 3
How can natural selection and inherited variations influence a population? Investigate factors that may have caused the variations in the European blackcaps.

 INTERACTIVITY

Evolution of the Blackcaps

In the 1960s, some European blackcaps started migrating to the United Kingdom from Central Europe during the winter. Over time, they have formed a distinct population of blackcaps.

IN LESSON 4

What can you learn from the fossil record? Think about how the fossil record of the European blackcap might provide information on how the bird has adapted over time.

Quest CHECK-IN

IN LESSON 5

What else would be helpful to know about European blackcaps? Research your questions and gather information to include in your report.

👆 **INTERACTIVITY**

Prepare Your Report

Quest FINDINGS

Complete the Quest!

Create a multimedia report about the two populations of European blackcaps and what caused them to be so different from each other.

👆 **INTERACTIVITY**

Reflect on Blackcap Migration

Walking Whales?

Background

Phenomenon Scientists have long believed that about 50 million years ago, the ancestors of modern whales had four legs and were similar to large dogs. Over time, they think whales evolved to become the giant marine mammals we recognize today. Scientists have had difficulty, however, finding fossils of whales that show how this dramatic change occurred. Recently, though, several new discoveries are helping scientists fill in the blanks in the evolutionary history of whales. Imagine that a paleontologist at a local university has been examining several fossils of animals that are thought to be ancestors of modern whales. She has invited your class to visit her laboratory and challenges you to order some of the early whale fossils from oldest to youngest.

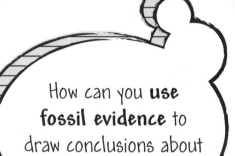

How can you **use fossil evidence** to draw conclusions about how whales evolved?

Materials

(per group)
- *Whales and Their Ancestors* handout
- scissors

Safety

Be sure to follow all safety procedures provided by your teacher. The Safety Appendix of your textbook provides more details about the safety icons.

Design a Procedure

1. From the handout, cut out the cards showing the orca and extinct ancestors of modern whales.

2. Develop a plan for how you can use the cards as evidence to support the following claim: **Modern whales evolved from ancestors that had four legs and were similar to large dogs.** Record your plan.

....
....
....
....
....

3. As you carry out your investigation, record any evidence you observe that modern whales have evolved over time.

Observations

HANDS-ON LAB

Connect Go online for a downloadable worksheet of this lab.

Analyze and Conclude

1. **SEP Interpret Data** Which whale ancestor do you think was the first to live most of its life in the water? Explain your thinking and support your response with evidence.

   ....
   ....
   ....
   ....

2. **SEP Construct Explanations** Based on your observations of the fossil remains of whale ancestors, what conditions in the environment do you think may have driven them to adapt to an aquatic environment over time?

   ....
   ....
   ....
   ....

3. **SEP Synthesize Information** Describe the overall pattern of physical, behavioral, and environmental changes you think took place in the evolutionary history of whales based on your sequence of fossils from oldest to youngest.

   ....
   ....
   ....
   ....
   ....
   ....
   ....
   ....
   ....

① Early Study of Evolution

Guiding Questions

- What processes explain how organisms can change over time?
- What observations and evidence support the theory of evolution?

Connection

Literacy Determine Central Ideas

MS-LS4-4

HANDS-ON LAB

ᴺInvestigate Model how species change over time.

Vocabulary

species
evolution
fossil
adaptation
scientific theory

Academic Vocabulary

hypothesize

Connect It !

✏ **Draw an arrow pointing to the squirrel that you think is better suited for the environment.**

SEP Construct Explanations Why do you think that squirrel is better suited for the environment? Explain your reasoning.

....

....

....

....

Observing Changes

Suppose you put a birdfeeder outside your kitchen or classroom window. You enjoy watching birds and gray squirrels come to get a free meal. The squirrels seem to be perfectly skilled at climbing the feeder and breaking open seeds. One day, you are surprised to see a white squirrel, like the squirrel in **Figure 1**, visiting the feeder. This new white squirrel and the gray squirrel appear to be the same **species**—a group of similar organisms that can mate with each other and produce offspring that can also mate and reproduce. You would probably have a few questions about where this squirrel came from and why it is white!

Curiosity About How Life Changes Scientists such as Charles Darwin were also curious about the differences they observed in natural populations. A variation is any difference between individuals of the same species. Some scientists asked how life on Earth got started and how it has changed over time throughout the planet's history. The scientists wondered what dinosaurs were like and why they disappeared. Darwin and others worked to develop a theory of **evolution**—the process by which modern organisms have descended from ancient organisms.

INTERACTIVITY

Explore feeding adaptations of animals in a coral reef ecosystem.

Surprise at the Birdfeeder!
Figure 1 In Brevard, North Carolina, about one-third of the Eastern gray squirrel population is white. In 1949, a resident received a pair of white squirrels as a gift. When one squirrel escaped, the other was released to join its friend. Soon after, people began to spot more white squirrels in town.

Organizing Life

Figure 2 Linnaeus classified life based on the structures of each organism.

Classify ✏ Identify three characteristics that you can observe in the image and list them below. Assign each characteristic a shape: a circle, square, or triangle. Using the characteristics you have identified, organize the organisms in the image into three groups by drawing the appropriate shapes around them.

....

....

....

....

....

....

....

....

....

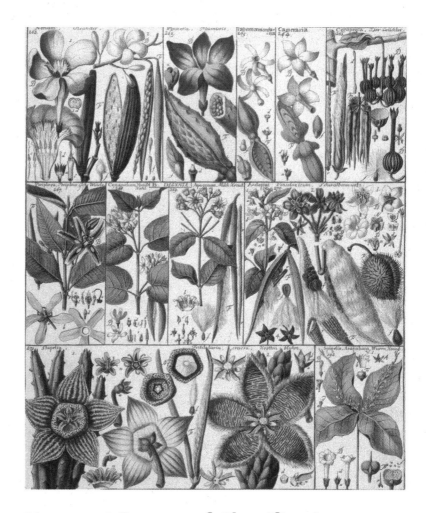

Make Meaning What problem or question have you had that required you to make observations and gather evidence to figure out?

Linnaeus' System of Classification

Recall that Carolus Linnaeus (1707–1778) developed the first scientific system for classifying and naming living things. Linnaeus collected samples of organisms from around the world. When classifying the organisms according to shared characteristics like those shown in **Figure 2**, he observed that there were variations of traits within a species. He was able to describe the variations and diversity of life, but not explain what caused that variation and diversity. No one was yet exploring how organisms came to be the way they are. In fact, many people still believed that organisms could appear out of the air as if by magic.

Lamarck's Idea

The first serious attempts to explain evolution began in the late 1700s. A French scientist, Jean-Baptiste Lamarck (1744–1829), was put in charge of a museum department of "Insects and Worms," which also included all the invertebrates, or animals without backbones. Lamarck devoted himself to learning everything he could about invertebrates. Unlike Linnaeus, Lamarck wasn't satisfied with describing what the animals looked like. Instead, Lamarck attempted to figure out how the organisms came to be. After much study, Lamarck developed the first attempt at a scientific theory of evolution.

Lamarck's Theory of Transformation Lamarck mistakenly believed that organisms could change during their lifetimes by selectively using or not using various parts of their bodies. For example, moles could develop long, strong claws by digging through dirt. Lamarck **hypothesized** that if two adult moles with long claws mated, their offspring would inherit those claws, as shown in **Figure 3**. In the next generation, the individuals who used their claws would pass even longer claws on to their offspring. In this way, the whole population of moles would gradually grow bigger, stronger claws, until they reached the form we see today.

Unfortunately, Lamarck's theory of transformation doesn't hold up when investigated further. His theory doesn't explain how features such as eyes could have developed. The theory also does not work when tested with experiments. For example, you can force a plant to grow sideways. However, the offspring of the plant grow straight up toward the light. While his theory was not correct, Lamarck did contribute some important new ideas. First, he suggested that evolution takes place by small, gradual steps. Second, he proposed that simple organisms could develop over many generations into more complex organisms.

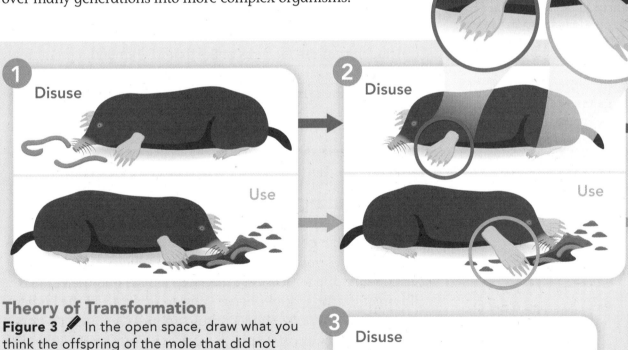

Theory of Transformation

Figure 3 🖉 In the open space, draw what you think the offspring of the mole that did not dig for food will look like, based on Lamarck's theory.

☑ READING CHECK **Draw Conclusions** Why was Lamarck's theory not supported?

....

....

....

Reading the Past

Figure 4 Charles Lyell discovered how to read Earth's history from layers of rock. Meanwhile, Mary Anning used fossils to reconstruct ancient animals.

1. **Interpret Photos** Examine the fossil. List the parts of the animal that you recognize. What kind of animal do you think this was?

....

....

....

2. **CCC Identify Patterns** Would you expect to find older or newer fossils in rock layers closer to the surface? Why?

....

....

....

....

....

Charles Lyell's Rocks Not long after Lamarck proposed his ideas, a young lawyer named Charles Lyell (1797–1875) began studying naturally-formed layers of rocks and fossils, like those in **Figure 4**. A **fossil** is the preserved remains or traces of an organism that lived in the past. Lyell concluded that the features of Earth had changed a great deal over time. He also stated that the processes that created land features in the past were still active. Before Lyell, some people estimated that the world was less than 6,000 years old. Lyell and other scientists pushed that estimate back more than 300 million years. Lyell's discoveries set the stage for a theory of gradual evolution over long periods of time.

Mary Anning's Fossils

Mary Anning (1799–1847) lived a much different life than Linnaeus, Lamarck, or Lyell. Coming from a poor family that made money by collecting fossils, Mary Anning would roam up and down the beach while searching for fossils in the steep cliffs along the English Channel. Anning taught herself how to reconstruct the bodies of fossilized animals. Many of these animals had never before been seen. Because of Anning's work, scientists began to realize that some animals had lived in the ancient past but no longer existed. While Anning had no formal training as a scientist, her observations and discoveries made her a key contributor in the study of both fossils and geology.

☑ **READING CHECK** **Summarize Text** How did the scientists show that organisms and Earth changed over time?

....

....

Darwin's Journey

In 1831, 22-year-old Charles Darwin set out on a five-year trip around the world aboard a British navy ship, the HMS *Beagle*. Darwin was a naturalist—a person who observes and studies the natural world. The captain of the *Beagle* wanted someone aboard who could make and record observations as the crew explored South America. One of Darwin's professors suggested inviting Darwin. And thus was launched a brilliant career!

Darwin was surprised to see the diversity of living things he encountered during the voyage. He saw insects that looked like flowers. He also saw armadillos digging insects from the ground. These mammals with a leathery shell that looks like a small suit of armor would have been very strange creatures to see. Today, scientists know that organisms are even more diverse than Darwin thought. Scientists have calculated that there are millions of species on Earth—and new ones are being identified all the time. Scientists have no way to estimate how many undiscovered species exist, but they believe the numbers are very high.

Fossils On his journey aboard the *Beagle*, Darwin also saw fossils of animals that had died long ago. Some of the fossils he observed confused him. **Figure 5** shows fossils Darwin found that resembled the bones of living armadillos but were much larger in size. Darwin wondered what had happened to the ancient, giant armadillos. Over long periods of time, could the giant armadillos have evolved into the smaller species we see today?

Armored Animals

Figure 5 Darwin thought that the fossil bones of giant Glyptodons (right) resembled the bones of modern armadillos (left).

1. **Determine Similarities** List two common features that the animals share.

   ....

   ....

2. **Infer** Why might these features be important to both ancient and modern armadillos?

   ....

   ....

   ....

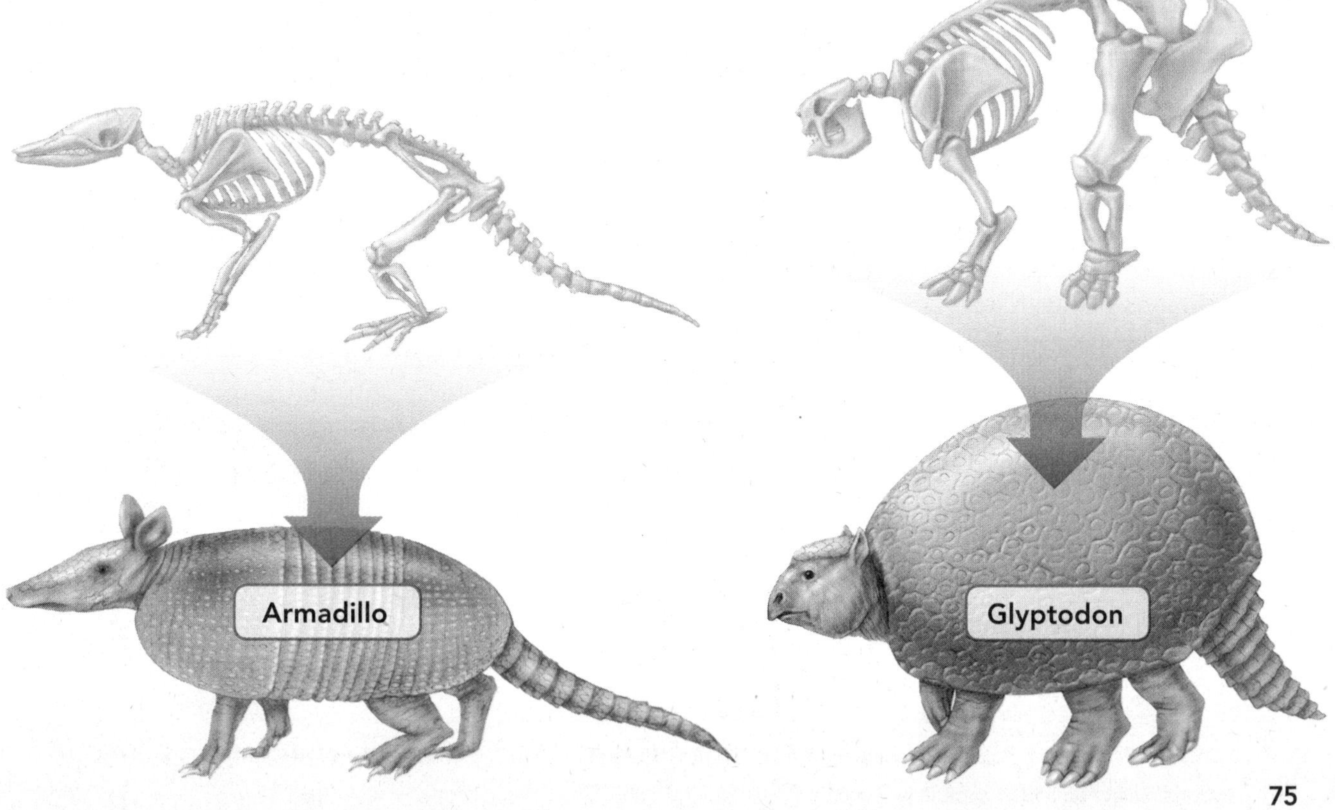

Armadillo

Glyptodon

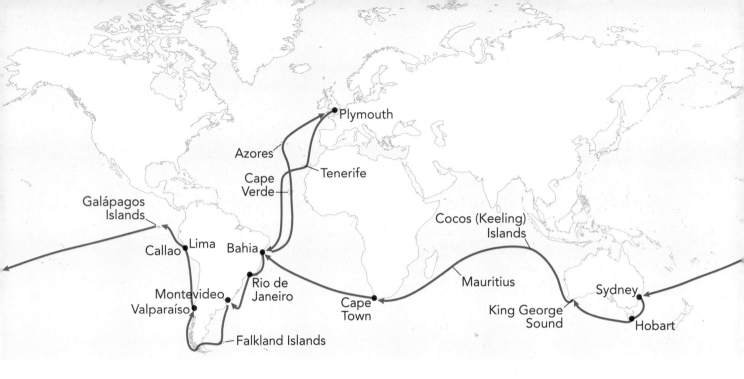

Voyage of the HMS *Beagle*, 1831–1836

Figure 6 Darwin sailed 40,000 miles around the world during his five-year voyage.

INTERACTIVITY

Observe organisms that Darwin encountered in the Galápagos Islands.

Long-Lost Relatives?

Figure 7  Mockingbirds on the South American mainland are similar to mockingbirds on the Galápagos Islands. Circle and label the features that are not similar.

CCC Relate Structure and Function Why do you think these birds have different traits?

....

....

....

....

Galápagos Organisms

The *Beagle* sailed to many different locations, as shown in **Figure 6**, and made several stops along the coast of South America. From what is now Ecuador on the Pacific coast, the ship traveled west to the Galápagos Islands. Darwin observed many different life forms there. He compared organisms from the Galápagos Islands to organisms that lived elsewhere. He also compared organisms living on the different islands.

Comparisons to the Mainland

Darwin discovered similarities between Galápagos organisms and those found in South America. Some of the birds and plants on the islands resembled those on the mainland. However, Darwin also noted important differences between the organisms. You can see differences between island and mainland mockingbirds in **Figure 7**. Darwin became convinced that species do not always stay the same. Instead, he thought species could change and even produce new species over time. Darwin began to think that the island species might be related to South American species. After much reflection, Darwin realized that the island species had become different from their mainland relatives over time.

Galápagos mockingbird

South American mockingbird

Comparisons Among the Islands Darwin collected birds from several of the Galápagos Islands. The birds were a little different from one island to the next. Darwin would learn that the birds were all types of finches. He concluded that the finch species were all related to a single common ancestor species that came from the mainland. Over time, different finches developed different beak shapes and sizes that were well suited to the food they ate. Beak shape is an example of an **adaptation**—an inherited behavior or physical characteristic that helps an organism survive and reproduce in its environment. Look at **Figure 8**. Birds with narrow, prying beaks can grasp insects. Those with long, pointed, sharp beaks can pick at cacti. Short, hooked beaks tear open fruit, while short, wide beaks crush seeds.

☑ READING CHECK **Determine Central Ideas** What convinced Darwin that species can change over time?

....

....

Question It !

We Got the Beak!
SEP Construct Explanations The finches in **Figure 8** show variations due to adaptation. Suppose someone asks you what caused a bird's beak to change to begin with. How would you answer the person?

....

....

....

....

Galápagos Finches
Figure 8 Darwin observed beak adaptations.

1. Claim Why is it necessary for finches to have different beaks?

....

....

....

....

....

2. Evidence 🖊 Draw an arrow from each finch matching it to the type of food you think it eats.

3. Reasoning Explain why your evidence supports your claim.

....

....

....

....

....

....

....

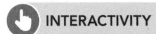

INTERACTIVITY

Identify plant and animal adaptations and how they help the organisms survive.

Literacy Connection

Determine Central Ideas
As you read, underline the elements that are needed to develop a scientific theory.

HANDS-ON LAB

☑**Investigate** Model how species change over time.

Darwin's Hypothesis Darwin thought about what he had observed during his voyage on the *Beagle*. By this time, while Darwin was convinced that organisms change over time, he wanted to know how the organisms changed. Darwin consulted other scientists and gathered more information. Based on his observations, Darwin reasoned that plants or animals that arrived on the Galápagos Islands faced conditions different from those on the nearby mainland. Darwin hypothesized that species change over many generations and become better adapted to new conditions. Darwin's hypothesis was an idea that contributed important new knowledge. Later, he and other scientists used it to test and develop a scientific theory.

Developing a Theory In science, a theory explains why and how things happen in nature. A **scientific theory** is a well-tested explanation for a wide range of observations and experimental results. Based on a body of facts, scientific theory is confirmed repeatedly through observation and experimentation. Darwin's ideas are often referred to as the theory of evolution. From the evidence he collected, and from all the discoveries of the scientists who had come before him, Darwin concluded that organisms on the Galápagos Islands had changed over time, or evolved.

☑ READING CHECK **Cite Textual Evidence** Why do you think theories, like Darwin's theory of evolution, are important to science?

....

....

....

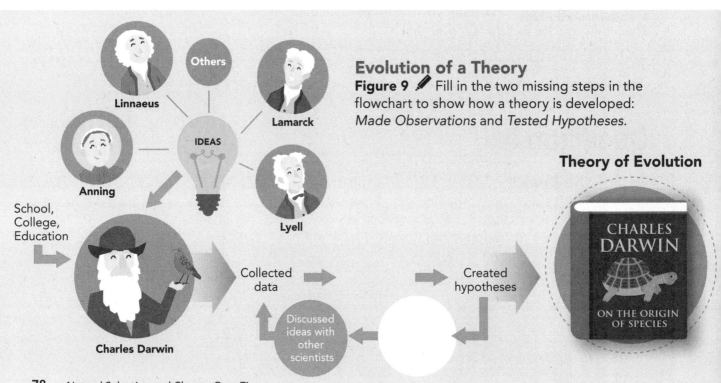

Evolution of a Theory
Figure 9 ✏ Fill in the two missing steps in the flowchart to show how a theory is developed: *Made Observations* and *Tested Hypotheses*.

Theory of Evolution

1. **Identify** Name four people, other than Darwin, whose work contributed to the study of evolution.

....

2. **Apply Scientific Reasoning** Why are fossils important to developing a theory of evolution?

....

....

....

3. **Compare and Contrast** How are variations and adaptations similar? How are they different?

....

....

....

....

....

4. **Integrate Information** Which two ideas of Lamarck contributed the most to Darwin's theory of evolution?

....

....

....

....

....

5. **SEP Construct Explanations** If the finches on the Galápagos Islands had such different beaks, how could Darwin think they shared a common ancestor from the mainland?

....

....

....

....

....

....

Quest CHECK-IN

In this lesson, you learned about adaptations and variations as well as the people whose ideas and activities contributed to understanding how organisms change over time. You also learned how Darwin developed his theory of evolution.

CCC Stability and Change Consider what you learned about variation and how species change over time. Why is it important to understand how a different migration route might be affecting the blackcaps' physical traits?

....

....

....

....

INTERACTIVITY

Meet the Blackcaps

Go online to draw conclusions about the variations between the two groups, based on what you've learned about where the birds migrate in winter.

Natural Selection

Guiding Questions

- How does natural selection lead to change over time in organisms?
- What are the roles of genes, mutations, and the environment in natural selection?

Connections

Literacy Cite Textual Evidence

Math Graph Proportional Relationships

MS-LS4-4, MS-LS4-5, MS-LS4-6

HANDS-ON LAB

и**Investigate** Measure variation in plant and animal populations.

Vocabulary

mechanism
natural selection
competition

Academic Vocabulary

expression

Connect It!

✏️ **Estimate how many dead fish are shown here. Write your estimation on the photograph.**

Explain Phenomena Some fish survived this event, known as a fish kill. What might be different about the fish that survived?

....

....

CCC Stability and Change If low oxygen levels occur every year and cause fish kills, how might the population of fish change over time?

....

Evolution by Natural Selection

Living in a small body of water can be dangerous for fish. If water conditions become unhealthy, there is nowhere for the fish to go. Too little rain, too many fish, and an overgrowth of algae can work together to reduce oxygen levels in water. **Figure 1** shows what happened when oxygen levels fell too low. A "fish kill" can wipe out most of the local population of a species of fish. Some individuals, however, usually survive the disaster. These fish will live to reproduce, thus ensuring the species survives.

Darwin's Search for a Mechanism After his return to England, Darwin was not satisfied with his theory of evolution. He struggled to determine evolution's mechanism. A **mechanism** is the natural process by which something takes place. Darwin asked himself how organisms could change over time. And how could a species become better adapted to new conditions? To solve this mystery, Darwin performed experiments and read the works of other naturalists and scientists.

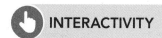
INTERACTIVITY

Identify how variations can impact squirrels.

Fish Kill
Figure 1 Fish can survive only in water with dissolved oxygen. When oxygen levels fall too low, thousands of fish can perish at once.

Rock dove
(*Columba livia*)

Fantail pigeon

Silky fantail pigeon

Fancy Pigeons

Figure 2 Through artificial selection, Darwin helped to create the fantail pigeon (center) from the wild rock dove, commonly known as a pigeon (left). Silky fantails (right) were then bred from the fantail pigeon.

Make Observations List the differences you see between the three different pigeon types.

Artificial Selection Darwin studied farm and pet animals produced by artificial selection. In artificial selection, only individuals with a desired trait, such as color, are bred by humans in the hope that the next generation will inherit the desired trait. Darwin himself bred pigeons with large, fan-shaped tails (see **Figure 2**). He repeatedly allowed only those pigeons with many tail feathers to mate. In this way, Darwin produced pigeons with two or three times the usual number of tail feathers. Darwin thought that a process similar to artificial selection might happen in nature. But he wondered what natural process performed the selection.

Natural Selection Darwin understood how evolution could work when he read an essay by Thomas Malthus. Malthus noted that both animals and humans can produce many offspring. If all the offspring survived, the world would quickly become overpopulated. There would not be enough food for everyone, and part of the population would starve. Darwin realized that some individuals have traits that help them to survive and reproduce. If these traits are hereditary, they can be passed on to the next generation. Gradually, over many generations, more and more individuals will have the helpful traits.

The Origin of Species Darwin waited a long time to publish his ideas. He thought they might be too revolutionary for the public to accept. Then, in 1858, Alfred Russel Wallace sent Darwin a letter. Wallace had also read Malthus' work and discovered the same mechanism for evolution! The next year, Darwin published his theory in *The Origin of Species*. In his book, Darwin proposed that evolution occurs by means of **natural selection**, a process by which individuals that are better adapted to their environment are more likely to survive and reproduce than other members of the same species.

How Natural Selection Works
Darwin identified three factors that affect the process of natural selection: overproduction, variaton, and competition. First, there must be overproduction, shown in **Figure 3** below. Darwin knew that most species produce more offspring than can possibly survive. Secondly, there must be variation. Members of a population differ from one another in many of their traits. For example, sea turtles may differ in color, size, the ability to crawl quickly on sand, and shell hardness. Such variations are hereditary, passed from parents to offspring through genetic material. Finally, there must be **competition**—the struggle among living things to get the necessary amount of food, water, and shelter. In many species, so many offspring are produced that there are not enough resources—food, water, and living space—for all of them.

☑ **READING CHECK** **Summarize** What are the factors that affect the process of natural selection?

HANDS-ON LAB

и**Investigate** Measure variation in plant and animal populations.

Overproduction
Figure 3 Brown rats can give birth up to 12 times each year with about 6 to 11 pups in each litter. The young rats are ready to breed when they are 12 weeks old.

1. **SEP Analyze Data** About how many pups can each female rat produce every year?

2. **Draw Conclusions** Why can't every rat survive and reproduce at its maximum rate?

Adaptations and Selection

Figure 4 Once sea turtles hatch from a nest, they must be fast and strong enough to reach the ocean before predators arrive.

Selection Darwin observed that some variations make individuals better adapted to their environment. Those individuals were more likely to survive and reproduce, and their offspring would inherit the helpful characteristic. The offspring, in turn, would be more likely to survive and reproduce and pass the characteristic to their offspring. After many generations, more members of the population would have the helpful characteristic. **Figure 4** shows an example of selection in a sea turtle population. In effect, conditions in the environment select the sea turtles with helpful traits to become parents of the next generation. Darwin proposed that, over a long time, natural selection can lead to change. Helpful variations may accumulate in a population, while unfavorable ones may disappear.

☑ **READING CHECK** **Cite Textual Evidence** Considering the environment, what helpful traits do you think would be passed on to increase the turtle population?

....

....

Math Toolbox

Hatching for Success

Sea turtles play an important role in maintaining Florida's coastal ecosystem.

1. Graph Proportional Relationships ✏ Complete the graph to compare the total number of sea turtle nests at each beach to the number of nests that hatched sea turtles. Create a key next to the graph.

2. SEP Construct Explanations On which beach(es) would you create a turtle refuge? Cite evidence to support your response.

....

....

....

Beach	Total Nests	Hatched Nests
Barefoot Beach	174	50
City of Naples	148	14
Delnor Wiggins	46	6
Marco Island	52	15
10,000 Islands	87	13

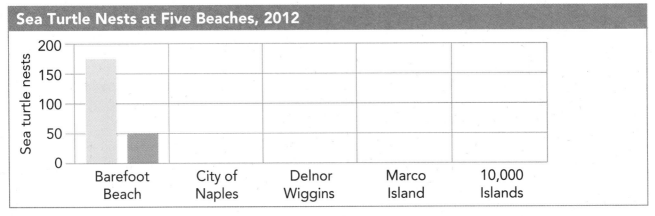

Sea Turtle Nests at Five Beaches, 2012

Environmental Change A change in the environment can affect an organism's ability to survive and may therefore lead to natural selection. For example, a storm can topple many trees in a forest. Trees that are better able to withstand strong winds have a survival advantage. In **Figure 5** you can see how natural selection might result in a shift in the population toward storm-resistant trees.

Model It

Natural Selection in Action

Figure 5 Natural events can lead to selection for favorable traits in a population. Read each image caption and use evidence to answer each question.

1990: Biologists survey a forest.

SEP Use Models List your observations related to the variation, competition, and overproduction of this tree population.

....

....

....

1991: Same forest after a windstorm.

Explain Phenomena What helpful trait did most of the surviving trees have?

....

....

....

2010: Same forest is surveyed again.

Make Observations How is the population different now compared to 1990?

....

....

2017: Another windstorm hits.

Develop Models ✏ In the space provided, draw the effect of the storm on the forest.

SEP Construct Explanations How will natural selection have changed the forest from 1990 to 2030?

....

....

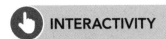
Genes and Natural Selection Darwin did a brilliant job of explaining natural selection, but he was never able to figure out where variations come from. He also did not understand how traits were passed from parents to offspring. Darwin hypothesized that tiny particles from around the parents' bodies passed into the developing offspring. Even at the time, Darwin realized that this explanation was flawed. Yet he did not have enough information to formulate a better explanation. You may recall Gregor Mendel and his study of heredity and genetics. Mendel's experiments in plant breeding took place during Darwin's life. His work showed that parents pass genes to their offspring. Genes are units of genetic material that provide instructions for a specific protein or function. Inherited variations result from individuals having different combinations of genes, as shown in **Figure 6**. Your hair color, eye color—and dimples, if you have them—are all determined by the genes your parents passed to you. Only traits controlled by genes can be acted upon by natural selection. Genetic variations contribute to the diversity of organisms.

Inherited Traits

Figure 6 Variations in traits depend on who the parents are.

1. **Make Observations** List several inherited variations you can observe in this group of students.

....
....
....
....
....
....
....
....
....
....
....

2. **CCC Cause and Effect** How did the students in **Figure 6** get such variations in traits?

....
....

Figure 7 A mutation caused the flower on the right to grow in an unusual way.

Explain Phenomena Describe how the mutation changed the flower.

....

....

....

Mutations Sexual reproduction causes existing gene variations to be recombined in each member of a population. To get a new variation, there must be a gene mutation. A mutation is any change to the genetic material. **Figure 7** shows a flower with an obvious mutation. Only mutations to reproductive cells can be passed on to offspring. In humans, new genetic variations are introduced by mutations to egg or sperm cells. A mutation to a body cell, such as a heart or brain cell, only affects the individual and is not passed on to offspring. If offspring are born with a mutation, natural selection will determine whether that mutation gets passed on to the next generation.

Epigenetic Changes Epigenetics is the study of small changes to DNA that turn genes on or off but do not change the genetic code itself. All the cells in your body have identical DNA, but functions vary greatly. Gene **expression** determines how a cell acts—whether it will function as a bone cell or a skin cell. In your lifetime, there will be small chemical changes to your DNA affecting how genes get expressed. Your offspring can inherit these changes.

Inherited changes can affect multiple generations. For example, smoking makes small changes to DNA. Due to epigenetics, a grandmother who smokes is more likely to have a grandchild with asthma. The grandchild will inherit the same epigenetic changes that smoking caused in his or her grandmother. Epigenetics is challenging the idea that natural selection acts on genetic variation alone. Scientists are working to understand how a gene that gets turned on or off in a body cell could show up two generations later.

INTERACTIVITY

Explore how a lack of genetic variations can impact crops.

Academic Vocabulary

Your friends may be able to tell what you are thinking based on your expression. How is a facial expression similar to gene expression?

....

....

....

....

....

☑ READING CHECK **Distinguish Facts** A mutation can be inherited only if it occurs in which type of cell?

....

☑ LESSON 2 Check

MS-LS4-4, MS-LS4-5, MS-LS4-6

1. Identify Darwin identified three factors affecting the process of natural selection. What are they?

....

2. Determine Differences The terms *mechanism* and *natural selection* both refer to natural processes. What makes them different?

....

....

....

....

3. Evaluate Claims A classmate claims that all mutations are both bad and inheritable. Is this true? Explain.

....

....

....

....

....

4. Apply Scientific Reasoning How does natural selection help a species to evolve?

....

....

....

5. SEP Construct Explanations How does the genetic variation of traits within a population affect its probability for survival? Explain.

....

....

....

....

....

....

6. CCC Cause and Effect Sea turtles can lay 50 to 200 eggs in a nest. Some eggs get destroyed or eaten by other animals. The young turtles that do hatch face many challenges as they head to the ocean. They may have to crawl up and down steep slopes, through seaweed, or around obstacles. Raccoons, foxes, crabs, birds, fish, and sharks may also eat them. Given the challenges and the data in the Math Toolbox, write an expression and use it to calculate the percent hatched. Use the percent to roughly estimate the number of sea turtles from a nest of 100 in Naples that reach the ocean safely. Express your answer as a percentage.

....

....

....

....

....

7. SEP Develop Models 🖊 Draw a young turtle and the variations you think could make it more successful. Label the variations and explain how they would benefit the turtle.

Fossils from Bedrock

VIDEO

Explore the techniques and technologies that scientists use to extract fossils.

Do you know how to get a fossil out of a rock? You engineer it! Scientists use several methods to extract these remains of the past.

The Challenge: To remove fossils from bedrock without damaging them or the surrounding area.

Phenomenon Fossils stay trapped under layers of rock for millions of years. When the geology of an area changes, these layers are sometimes exposed. This offers a great opportunity to search for evidence of how adaptation by natural selection contributes to the evolution of a species.

Removing a fragile fossil from rock takes skill, time, and special tools. Sometimes fossil collectors have to dig out the larger section of rock holding a fossil. Until recently, extracting a fossil meant slowly and carefully chipping away at the rock with a small chisel and hammer, then sweeping away rock dust with a small brush. The latest technology is the pneumatic drill pen. Vibrating at 30,000 times each minute, the drill pen carves out a fossil more quickly and with greater control. Another method is the acid wash. While it takes much longer than the mechanical methods, and can only be used on fossils found in limestone and chalk, an acid wash is the safest way to remove a fossil.

Scientists carefully brush away dirt and debris from bones discovered in dig sites to gather fossil evidence of how organisms have changed over time.

DESIGN CHALLENGE

How would you modify the process for removing fossils from bedrock? Go to the Engineering Design Notebook to find out!

Guiding Questions

- How do natural selection and inherited variations influence a population?
- How does sexual selection influence a population's genetic variation?
- How is species interaction a factor in evolution?

Connection

Literacy Determine Conclusions

MS-LS4-4, MS-LS4-6

HANDS-ON LAB

uInvestigate Explore how different birds' feet help them survive in their environments.

Vocabulary

fitness
sexual selection
coevolution

Academic Vocabulary

randomly
interactions

Connect It!

✏️ **Label each duck as either male or female.**

CCC Structure and Function Do you think that both ducks' appearance could be a result of natural selection? Explain your reasoning.

....

....

....

Processes of Evolution

Charles Darwin's theory of natural selection is straightforward. Any population of living things has inherited variations. In addition, the population produces more young than can survive. According to natural selection, only the individuals that are well-adapted to their environments will survive and reproduce. An organism's **fitness** describes how well it can survive and reproduce in its environment. According to Darwin's theory, the fittest individuals survive to reproduce and pass their traits to the next generation. Organisms with low fitness are not as well-adapted to their environment and may die without reproducing or may not have as many offspring. Over time, as individual organisms successfully respond to changing conditions in the environment, the population evolves and its fitness increases.

Beyond Natural Selection Observe the male and female mandarin ducks in **Figure 1**. Both ducks have many adaptations that help them survive and reproduce in their watery habitat. Oily feathers keep the ducks dry. Webbed feet propel the ducks quickly through the water. Nesting in trees keeps ducklings safe from predators. Dull colors help the female duck blend in with her background. Now, look at the male duck. He seems to be calling for attention! His brightly colored face and the bold black and white stripes on his sides surely attract predators. How could natural selection result in traits that hurt the male duck's chance of survival? Answer: There is more to evolution than "survival of the fittest."

HANDS-ON LAB

Investigate Explore how different birds' feet help them survive in their environments.

Opposites Attract
Figure 1 Believe it or not, these ducks are both from the same species. Male and female mandarin ducks have evolved to look very different!

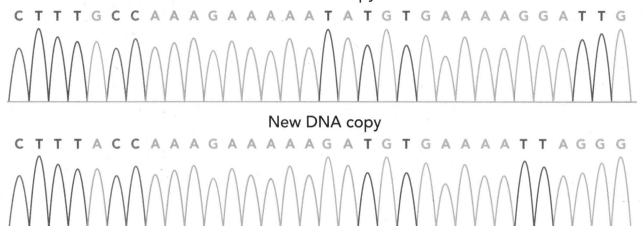

Old DNA copy

C T T T G C C A A A G A A A A A T A T G T G A A A A G G A T T G

New DNA copy

C T T T A C C A A A G A A A A A G A T G T G A A A A T T A G G G

Spellcheck, Please!

Figure 2 ✏ A mutation is like a spelling error in a gene's DNA sequence of nucleotides—A, C, G, and T. Any change in the sequence results in a mutation. Here, each nucleotide has its own color. Observe how the sequence of nucleotides changes. Compare the sequences of the two DNA copies. Circle any differences you observe in the new DNA copy.

Explain Phenomena   What do you think may have caused the differences between the two DNA copies?

....

....

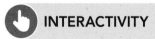

INTERACTIVITY

Analyze mutations and how they can impact evolution.

Mutations One reason for Darwin's oversimplification of evolution was that he did not yet know about mutations. You've already learned that a mutation is any change to an organism's genetic material. Mutations can create multiple alleles, or forms of a gene. Different alleles cause variations in traits such as eye color, ear shape, and blood type.

How Mutations Happen Mutations are created in two ways. First, a dividing cell can make an error while copying its DNA (see **Figure 2**). There are approximately six billion units in one copy of human DNA. Imagine copying by hand a book that had six billion letters. Think how easy it would be to make a mistake! Researchers estimate that each human child inherits an average of 60 new mutations from his or her parents. That sounds like a lot, doesn't it? But it means that the body makes only one mistake out of every 100 million units of DNA copied. Secondly, mutations also occur when an organism is exposed to environmental factors such as radiation or certain chemicals that damage the cell's DNA. While the cell has mechanisms to repair damaged DNA, that repair is not always perfect. Any mistake while fixing the DNA results in a mutation.

Effects of Mutations Most mutations have no effect on the individual organism. The mutation may be in a part of the DNA that is inactive. Or the mutation may not cause a difference in the function of the body. Out of the mutations that do affect function, most are harmful to the individual. **Randomly** changing a process in the body typically results in decreased function. Only mutations to sex cells can get passed on and affect the fitness of offspring. A mutation that increases fitness tends to grow more common in a population. A mutation that decreases fitness tends to disappear because the individuals with that mutation die or reproduce less successfully.

Need for Mutations People often think of mutations as harmful. It's true that mutations can lead to cancer and genetic defects. At the same time, however, mutations are necessary for evolution to occur. Mutations create all the variations among members of a species and account for the diversity of organisms on Earth. **Figure 3** shows how mutations can change plant leaf shapes. Imagine if the first single-celled organisms had never experienced mutation! That first species would have been the only life that ever existed on the planet.

☑ **READING CHECK** **Summarize Text** How are mutations both harmful and helpful?

....

....

Academic Vocabulary

List where you may have heard the word *random* used before. What does *randomly* mean as it's used here?

....

....

....

....

....

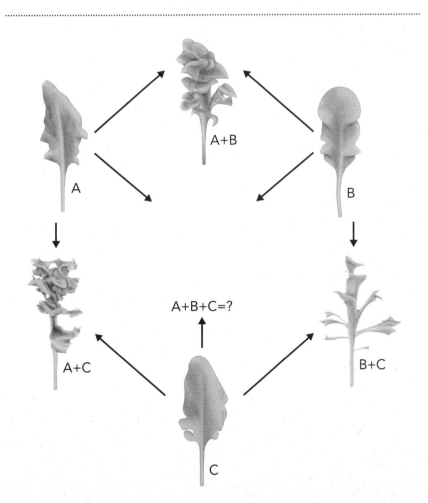

Variations from Mutations

Figure 3 Scientists studied how three mutations in mustard plant DNA (labeled A, B, and C in the image) affect leaf shape.

SEP Use a Model to Predict 🖉 Examine the effects of the mutations on leaf shape. In the center of the image, draw what you think the leaves would look like if a plant had all three mutations.

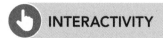

INTERACTIVITY

Investigate how populations of organisms evolve due to gene flow and genetic drift.

Gene Flow Mutations are not the only source of new alleles in a population. Alleles also enter a population through gene flow. As you know, a gene is a unit of genetic material that acts as instructions for a specific protein or function. Gene flow occurs when individuals with new alleles physically move from one population to another. Gene flow can increase the genetic variation of a population.

How do individuals move between populations? Sometimes birds and insects are blown to a new continent by a storm. Plant seeds and pollen can stick to animal fur and travel long distances, too. Humans are often accidentally responsible for gene flow. Animals, seeds, and microorganisms can hitch a ride on trucks or in the water in the bottom of ships.

Genetic Drift The last mechanism of evolution is a random, directionless process. Just by chance, some alleles may be lost to a population. Think of a small population of birds living on an island. The only bird that carries an allele for light-colored feathers could be hit by lightning and die. It will pass no genes on to the next generation. Through random chance, the genetic variation of the population shrinks over time. This process is called genetic drift. **Figure 4** shows how gene flow and genetic drift affect the level of variation in a population of snakes.

☑ READING CHECK **Determine Central Ideas** How do gene flow and genetic drift play a role in evolution?

....

....

....

Gene Flow and Genetic Drift

Figure 4 ✏ Examine how snakes enter or leave the snake population in each of the images and label the process taking place as either *genetic drift* or *gene flow.*

Original Snake Population

Process: ....

Process: ....

Male Competition
Figure 5 Stag beetles compete to control the best territory. A good territory gives the winning beetle access to females for mating.

1. Identify ✎ Circle the feature of the beetles that has grown due to male competition.

2. CCC Structure and Function Do you think that female stag beetles also have the same large feature?

....

....

....

....

....

....

Sexual Selection

The measure of an individual's fitness is its ability to survive and reproduce. An organism that reproduces asexually can reproduce all on its own. An organism that reproduces sexually, however, must blend its genes with those of a mate. **Sexual selection** is natural selection that acts on an organism's ability to get the best possible mate. The fitness of the offspring depends on the fitness of both the parents. Therefore, sexually-reproducing organisms try to choose mates with specific traits that have higher fitness.

Female Choice In some species, females choose which males will father their offspring. Natural selection favors traits that help females choose mates with high fitness. Consider the ducks in **Figure 1**. Suppose that male ducks with bright feathers have better fitness. Females may evolve a trait that causes them to choose males with bright feathers. Over time, male ducks will grow brighter and fancier feathers. Even after the bright colors start to hurt the males' survival, the females may continue to select males with ever-brighter feathers.

Male Competition In other species, males compete to control a territory with access to females. Any trait that gives males an advantage in the competition will be favored by natural selection. Male competition can lead to exaggerated horns, pincers, or body size, as shown in **Figure 5**. The need to reproduce can cause males to evolve characteristics that make them less likely to survive!

✓ READING CHECK **Determine Conclusions** Why do you think bright feathers make a male duck a desirable mate?

....

....

....

📓 **Reflect** What is a difference that you have observed between male and female members of the same species in a zoo, aquarium, or in your local community?

Coevolution and Cooperation

Figure 6 The acacia tree and ants both evolved features that help them work together.

Infer What features do you think the acacia tree and the ants might have that would help one another?

....

....

....

....

....

Academic Vocabulary

If you break down the word *interactions*, it means "the actions between." How would you define interactions between two species?

....

....

....

....

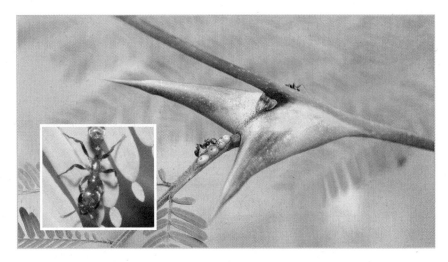

Coevolution

Two or more species with close **interactions** can affect each other's evolution. **Coevolution** is the process by which two species evolve in response to changes in each other over time. Coevolution can happen when species cooperate with each other, as shown in **Figure 6**. Several acacia trees in Central America have coevolved with select species of ants. The acacias trees evolved hollow thorns and nectar pores because of their close interactions with the ants. Likewise, the ants evolved defense behaviors to protect "their" trees. A queen ant lays her eggs in the hollow thorns of an acacia tree. In return for the shelter and food from the tree, the ants protect the tree. They attack when other insects or animals try to devour the acacia leaves. Other examples of interactions that can lead to coevolution include species that compete for resources and species involved in a prey-predator relationship.

Mimicry in Coevolution

Figure 7 Tiger-wing butterflies evolved to absorb and store toxins from plants they ate when they were caterpillars. This makes them taste bad. Birds avoid eating tiger-wing butterflies and other butterflies that mimic, or closely resemble, them.

SEP Develop Models ✏ Sketch the progression of how a butterfly's wing patterns may have changed over time to mimic that of the tiger-wing butterfly.

MS-LS4-4, MS-LS4-6

1. SEP Communicate Information What does fitness mean in terms of evolution?

....

....

2. SEP Cite Evidence How does gene flow affect a population's genetic variation?

....

....

3. Apply Concepts Is sexual selection a form of natural selection? Explain.

....

....

....

....

4. Apply Scientific Reasoning What are the two ways in which mutations are created? Give at least one example of an environmental factor.

....

....

....

....

5. SEP Construct Explanations Explain the role of mutations in genetic variation and in the diversity of living things. Support your explanation with evidence.

....

....

....

....

....

....

....

....

6. Explain Phenomena How is species interaction a factor in evolution? Use the ant and the acacia tree as an example.

....

....

....

....

Quest CHECK-IN

In this lesson, you learned how a population can be influenced by natural selection, species interactions, and genetic variations due to mutations, gene flow, genetic drift, and sexual selection.

CCC Cause and Effect Is it important to consider the role of genetic variations when trying to determine what caused the changes to the European blackcaps?

....

....

....

....

....

INTERACTIVITY

Evolution of the Blackcaps

Go online to investigate factors that may have caused the variations in the European blackcaps.

Evidence in the Fossil Record

Guiding Questions

- What supports evidence for the scientific theory of evolution?
- How do fossils show change over time?
- What does the early development of different organisms tell us about evolution?
- How does failure to adapt to a changing environment lead to a species' extinction?

Connections

Literacy Summarize Text

Math Analyze Proportional Relationships

MS-LS4-1, MS-LS4-2, MS-LS4-3, MS-LS4-6

HANDS-ON LAB

иInvestigate Model how different fossils form.

Vocabulary

fossil record
embryo
homologous
 structures
extinct

Academic Vocabulary

evidence

Connect It!

✏ **Draw arrows to connect similar features between the fossil and the modern animal.**

SEP Obtain, Evaluate, and Communicate Information Which parts of the crinoid's tentacles are best preserved in the fossils? Which parts were not preserved?

....

....

....

The Fossil Record

Fossils are preserved remains or traces of living things. **Figure 1** shows fossils of crinoids, relatives of modern-day starfish. All the fossils that have been discovered and what we have learned from them make up the **fossil record**. The patterns in the fossil record are like data that scientists can analyze and interpret. The fossil record documents the diversity of the life forms, many now extinct, and shows how life forms existed and changed throughout Earth's history. The fossil record is a treasure trove of **evidence** about how organisms of the past evolved into the forms we see today.

Microevolution and Macroevolution
Scientists can observe evolution taking place within populations of organisms. Small, gradual changes in the color or size of a certain population is called microevolution. *Micro-* means very small, and *evolution* means change through time. One example of microevolution is the northern population of house sparrows. They adapted to a colder climate by growing larger bodies than the southern population. This small change took less than 100 years. Usually, for multicellular organisms, it takes years to thousands of years for a new species to develop. Scientists turn to the fossil record to learn about macroevolution, or major evolutionary change.

Academic Vocabulary
Where have you read or heard the word *evidence* used before? List at least one synonym for *evidence*.

....

....

....

....

A Glimpse of the Past
Figure 1 Crinoids are relatives of starfish. We can learn a lot about the evolution of crinoids by looking at fossils of their extinct relatives. Some ancient crinoids grew more than 40 meters long!

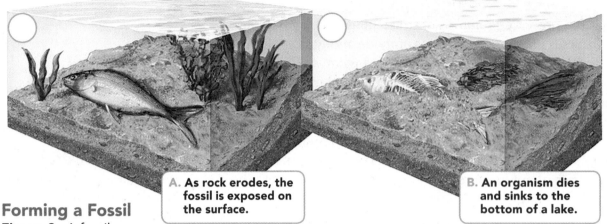

A. As rock erodes, the fossil is exposed on the surface.

B. An organism dies and sinks to the bottom of a lake.

Forming a Fossil

Figure 2 A fossil may form when sediment quickly covers a dead organism.

Relate Text to Visuals
🖊 Are the images matched with the correct captions? Or are there some mistakes? Match up each image with the right caption by writing the correct letters in the blank circles.

How Fossils Form
A fossil is the impression that an organism or part of an organism leaves in rock. That impression comes about in one of two ways. A mold creates a hollow area in the rock that is the shape of an organism or part of an organism. Or, a cast makes a solid copy of an organism's shape, sometimes containing some of the original organism.

Most fossils form when living things die and sediment buries them. Sediment is the small, solid pieces of material that come from rocks or the remains of organisms and settle to the bottom of a body of water. Over time, the sediment slowly hardens into rock and preserves the shapes of the organisms. Fossils can form from any kind of living thing, from bacteria to dinosaurs.

Many fossils come from organisms that once lived in or near still water. Swamps, lakes, and shallow seas build up sediment quickly and bury remains of living things. In **Figure 2**, you can see how a fossil might form. When an organism dies, its soft parts usually decay quickly or are eaten by other organisms. Only hard parts of an organism typically leave fossils. These hard parts include bones, shells, teeth, seeds, and woody stems. It is rare for the soft parts of an organism to become a fossil. People often see fossils after erosion exposes them. Erosion is the wearing away of Earth's surface by natural processes such as water and wind.

Many Kinds of Fossils

Figure 3 A fossil may be the preserved remains of an organism's body, or the trace of an organism—something it leaves behind.

1. **Classify** 🖊 Label each image as either a body fossil or a trace fossil.

2. **SEP Evaluate Evidence** Why did you classify them that way?

....
....
....
....
....
....

Snail shells

Turtle dropping

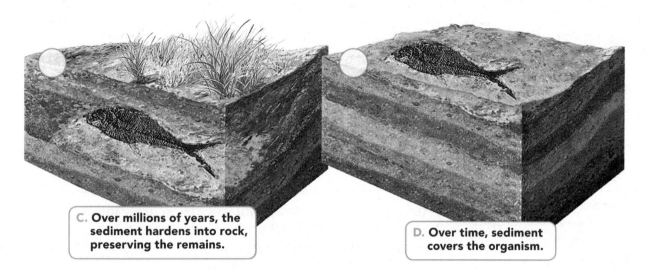

C. Over millions of years, the sediment hardens into rock, preserving the remains.

D. Over time, sediment covers the organism.

Kinds of Fossils There are two types of fossils: body fossils and trace fossils. Each one gives us different information about the ancient organism it represents.

Body Fossils Body fossils preserve the shape and structure of an organism. We can learn about what a plant or animal looked like from a body fossil. Body fossils of trees are called petrified wood. The term *petrified* means "turned into stone." Petrified fossils are fossils in which minerals replace all or part of an organism. In petrified wood, the remains are so well preserved that scientists can often count the rings to tell how old a tree was when it died millions of years ago. Ancient mammoths frozen into ice, petrified dinosaur bones, and insects trapped in amber are other examples of body fossils.

Trace Fossils We can learn what an animal did from trace fossils. Footprints, nests, and animal droppings preserved in stone are all trace fossils, as shown in **Figure 3**.

HANDS-ON LAB

Investigate Model how different fossils form.

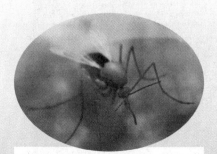

Mosquito in amber

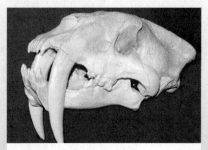

Smilodon, cat skull

Dinosaur tracks

INTERACTIVITY

Analyze data and look for patterns in the fossil record.

Literacy Connection

Summarize Text At the end of each two-page spread, stop to see if you can summarize what you just read.

Fossil Evidence of Evolution

Most of what we know about ancient organisms comes from the fossil record. The fossil record provides evidence about the history of life and past environments on Earth. The fossil record also shows how different groups of organisms have changed over time. Each new discovery helps to fill holes in our understanding of evolution.

Early Earth When Earth first formed, more than 4.5 billion years ago, it was extremely hot. Earth was likely mostly melted. As Earth cooled, solid rocks became stable at Earth's surface. The oldest known fossils are from rocks that formed about a billion years after Earth formed. **Figure 4** shows a rock made of these fossils. Scientists think that all other forms of life on Earth arose from these simple organisms.

Scientists cannot yet pinpoint when or where life first evolved. Scientists hypothesize that life first evolved in Earth's ocean. The early ocean contained reactive chemicals. Under the right conditions, sunlight and lightning can change those chemicals into molecules similar to those found in living cells. More research will help scientists to settle the question of the origin of life on Earth.

Fossils Reveal Early Life
Figure 4 Stromatolites are rock-like structures formed by layers of fossilized bacteria. Dating as far back as 3.4 billion years ago, they are the oldest evidence of life forms on Earth. Ancient bacteria in water produced thin sheets of film that trapped mud. Over time, these thin sheets formed microfossils—fossils too small to see without a microscope. Eventually, the sheets built up into the layers you see here.

Interpret Photos ✏ Draw a scale next to the fossil stromatolite to show which are the oldest layers and which are the youngest.

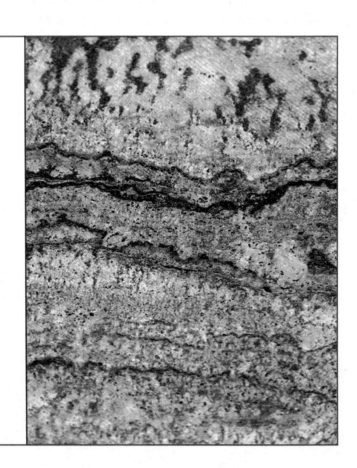

Gomphotherium
24–5 mya

Moeritherium
36 mya

Platybelodon
23–5.3 mya

Mammut americanum
(American mastodon)
4 mya–11,500 ya

Mammuthus
(Woolly Mammoth)
Pliocene, from
750,000–11,500 ya

Loxodonta
(African elephant)
1.8 mya–present

ya = years ago; mya = millions of years ago

Fossils and Evolution Through Time The fossil record provides evidence that life on Earth has evolved. Rock forms in layers, with newer layers on top of older layers. When we dig deeper, we see older rocks with fossils from earlier time periods. The oldest rocks contain fossils of only very simple organisms. Younger rocks include fossils of both simple organisms and also more complex organisms. Looking at fossils in rocks from different time periods, scientists can reconstruct the history of evolution. **Figure 5** shows the evolution of the elephant, reconstructed from the fossil record.

The fossil record also shows how Earth's climate has changed. Some plant fossils reveal surprises, such as palm trees in Wyoming and giant tropical ferns in Antarctica. Fossils and preserved remains are also evidence of how climate change influences evolution.

Evolution of the Modern Elephant
Figure 5 Scientists have reconstructed the evolutionary history of the elephant with evidence from the fossil record.

☑ READING CHECK
Determine Conclusions
Would you expect to find fossils related to the evolution of the elephant in the oldest rocks in the fossil record? Why?

....

....

....

Question It !

Kyle has very limited vision and needs someone to explain the evolution of elephants to him. Suppose you are going to work with Kyle to help him understand the changes elephants have undergone.

Interpret Diagrams Using **Figure 5**, what features of the animals have stayed the same? What features have changed?

....

....

....

....

....

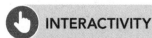
INTERACTIVITY

Analyze and compare the structure and development of embryos to determine evolutionary relationships.

Comparisons of Anatomy

The structure of an organism's body is called its anatomy. Similarities in anatomy are clues that organisms evolved from a common ancestor. Evidence from the fossil record and observations of modern organisms help us to reconstruct evolutionary history.

Embryological Development

An **embryo** is a young organism that develops from a fertilized egg (called a zygote). The growing embryo may develop inside or outside the parent's body. The early development of different organisms in an embryo shows some striking similarities. For example, chickens, fish, turtles, and pigs all resemble each other during the early stages of development. These similarities in early development suggest that organisms are related and share a common ancestor.

Scientists can also analyze fossilized eggs to learn about development in species from long ago. **Figure 6** shows the model of a duck-billed dinosaur embryo, known as a Hadrosaur, compared to an x-ray of a chicken embryo. You can see many similarities in their early development.

Homologous Structures

Similar structures that related species have inherited from a common ancestor are known as **homologous structures** (hoh MAHL uh gus). Bats, dogs, dolphins, and even flying reptiles have homologous structures in their limbs. Although the structures look very different now, in the Math Toolbox you can see the bones that these animals all have in common.

✔ READING CHECK **Determine Conclusions** If two organisms have homologous structures and similar early development, what can you infer about them?

....

....

INTERACTIVITY

Examine patterns of anatomical similarities and differences among organisms.

Birds and Dinosaurs

Figure 6 🖊 Draw lines and label the features that look similar in both the Hadrosaur and chicken embryos.

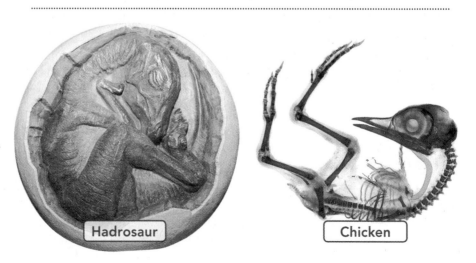

Hadrosaur   Chicken

Homologous Anatomical Structures

The wings, flipper, and leg of these organisms all have similar anatomical (body) structures. Note that the structures are not drawn to scale.

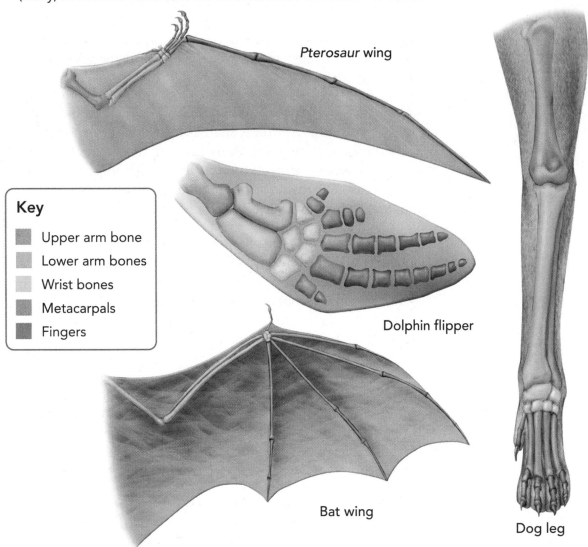

Pterosaur wing

Key

- Upper arm bone
- Lower arm bones
- Wrist bones
- Metacarpals
- Fingers

Dolphin flipper

Bat wing

Dog leg

1. **Construct Tables** ✏ Choose two of the animals shown above to examine closely. Using a metric ruler, measure the upper arm bone, the lower arm bone, and the fingers. Create a data table at right and record the measurements in millimeters.

2. **CCC Analyze Proportional Relationships** In each species, compare the upper arm to lower arm, or compare fingers to metacarpals. Can you find any equivalent ratios?

....

....

....

....

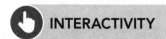

INTERACTIVITY

Interpret data from the fossil record that supports species extinction.

Beginning and End of a Species

Natural selection explains how variations can lead to changes in a species. A new species forms when one population remains isolated from the rest of its species long enough to evolve such different traits that members of the two populations can no longer mate and produce offspring capable of reproduction. **Figure 7** shows an example of a turtle species that has evolved seven different subspecies. Over time, the subspecies could form separate species.

Gradual Change Some species in the fossil record seem to change gradually over time, such as the elephants in **Figure 5**. The time scale of the fossil record involves thousands or millions of years. There is plenty of time for gradual changes to produce new species. The fossil record contains many examples of species that are halfway between two others.

Rapid Change At times, new, related species suddenly appear in the fossil record. Rapid evolution can follow a major change in environmental conditions. A cooling climate, for example, can put a lot of stress on a population. Only the individuals adapted to cooler conditions will survive. Through natural selection, the population may rapidly evolve to a new species.

Extinction A species is **extinct** if it no longer exists and will never again live on Earth. A rapid environmental change is more likely to cause a species to become extinct than to bring about a new species. The fossil record shows that most of the species that ever lived on Earth are now extinct.

New predators, climate change, disease, and competition with other species are a few factors that can lead to extinction. According to natural selection, if a species fails to develop the adaptations necessary to survive the changing conditions in an environment, that species will not survive and reproduce. Small populations that breed slowly and cannot relocate are more likely to become extinct. The fossil record shows that volcanic eruptions, asteroids striking Earth, and sudden climate change can kill off many species in a short time.

☑ READING CHECK **Translate Information** How do you know that the animals whose limbs are depicted in the Math Toolbox had a common ancestor at one point? What question could you ask to find out more and why would you ask it?

....

....

....

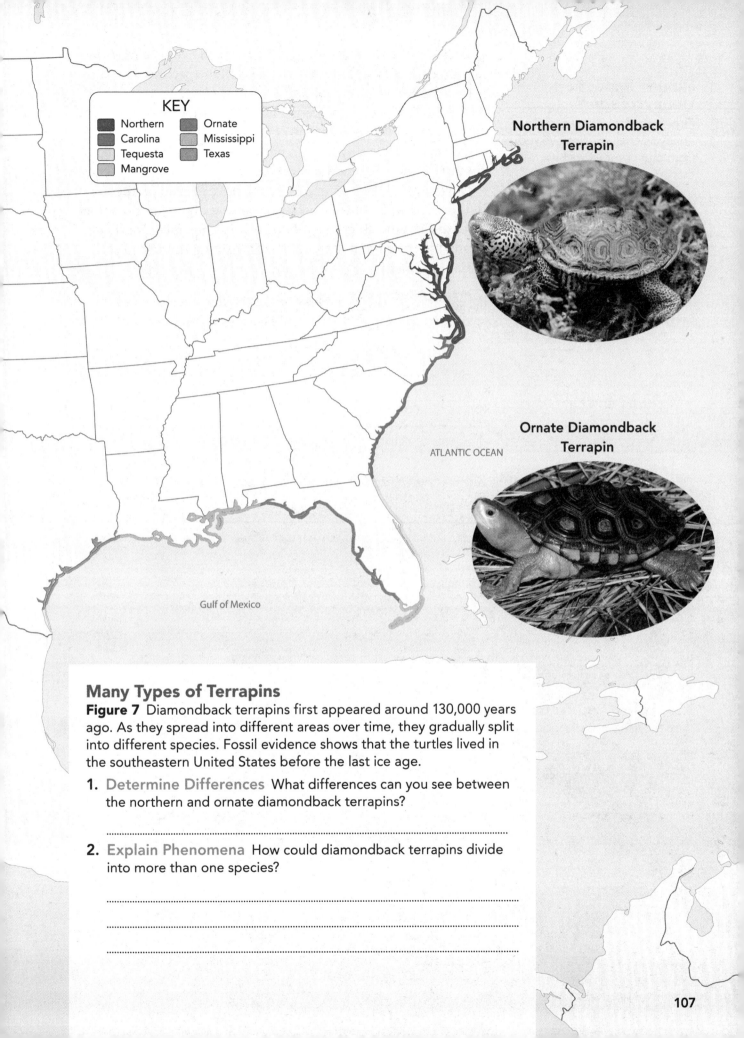

KEY
- Northern
- Carolina
- Tequesta
- Mangrove
- Ornate
- Mississippi
- Texas

Northern Diamondback Terrapin

Ornate Diamondback Terrapin

ATLANTIC OCEAN

Gulf of Mexico

Many Types of Terrapins

Figure 7 Diamondback terrapins first appeared around 130,000 years ago. As they spread into different areas over time, they gradually split into different species. Fossil evidence shows that the turtles lived in the southeastern United States before the last ice age.

1. **Determine Differences** What differences can you see between the northern and ornate diamondback terrapins?

   ....

2. **Explain Phenomena** How could diamondback terrapins divide into more than one species?

   ....

   ....

   ....

Human Impact on Honeycreepers

Figure 8 Many Hawaiian honeycreeper species evolved from one or more finches that traveled to the islands thousands of years ago. Most honeycreeper species are now extinct or endangered.

Construct Explanations How could the honeycreepers' island habitat make them more likely to go extinct?

....

....

....

....

Human Influence on Extinction Some extinctions are direct results of human activities. Other species struggle to survive human-caused pollution, such as oil spills. Many scientists think we are currently living in a time period of rapid extinction. A large percentage of the species on Earth could be driven to extinction by human activities and human-caused climate change. **Figure 8** shows some of the estimated 56 species of Hawaiian honeycreepers known to have existed on the islands. Today, all but 18 species are now extinct. Rat predators, disease-carrying chickens, malaria-laden mosquitos, and pigs trampling their habitat are all factors driving these tropical birds to extinction.

✓ **READING CHECK** **Summarize Text** What causes a new species to develop and what causes a species to go extinct?

....

....

....

☑LESSON 4 Check

MS-LS4-1, MS-LS4-2, MS-LS4-3, MS-LS4-6

1. Determine Differences What sort of information can you get from a body fossil that you can't get from a trace fossil?

....

....

....

2. SEP Analyze Data According to the fossil record, which level in the rock layers shown in the diagram will have the oldest organisms? Explain.

....

....

....

....

....

....

3. SEP Construct Explanations How do you account for differences between the bat's wing and the dolphin's flipper?

....

....

....

....

Dolphin flipper

Bat wing

4. SEP Engage in Argument What can you say to back the claim that the fossil record supports the theory of evolution?

....

....

....

....

5. CCC Describe Patterns If you were a scientist trying to determine if an organism evolved gradually or rapidly, how would patterns in the fossil record help you? Explain how the pattern would provide evidence to support the rate of evolution for that organism.

....

....

....

....

....

....

....

....

....

....

....

6. Apply Scientific Reasoning Why is a sudden change in the environment more likely to cause a species to go extinct rather than to cause a new species to develop?

....

....

....

....

....

....

....

Could DINOSAURS Roar?

Vegavis is not the direct ancestor of modern-day ducks or chickens, but it is closely related to waterfowl such as geese.

So many movies have dinosaurs roaring as they roam across the landscape shredding trees and devouring prey the size of SUVs. Fossil evidence, however, supports a more silent world. In fact, it wasn't until about 65 to 68 million years ago that a very important piece of anatomy developed—the syrinx. Think of it as a voice box.

In 1992, on an Antarctic island, scientists found a fossil of *Vegavis iaai*, a bird that lived between 68 and 65 million years ago. At that time in Earth's history, Antarctica had a tropical climate. It wasn't until recently that technology revealed the most important find in the fossil: a syrinx.

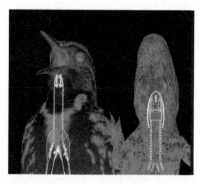

Location of syrinx in living songbird compared to larynx in an alligator

The presence of a syrinx in the *Vegavis iaai* fossil strongly suggests that the bird was capable of producing sounds. In the songbird, as in *Vegavis*, the syrinx is located in the chest. In the alligator, the larynx is located in the throat.

Photo Credit: Dr. Julia Clarke, University of Texas at Austin

Connections to Modern-Day Birds

The presence of a syrinx helps us to understand the ancestry of modern birds. Because of the asymmetrical structure of the syrinx, scientists speculate that the bird may have honked like a goose. Scientists analyzed the same structures in 12 living birds and compared them to the next oldest fossilized syrinx that was available. They found similarities in structure across the samples. Their findings supported the claim that *Vegavis iaai* was related to modern birds, but not an ancestor of modern reptiles, who are also able to vocalize through the larynx.

It would take a large brain to produce a selection of noises that meant something. If dinosaurs were able to vocalize or utter any sounds at all, then the sounds they made would have been a far cry from what you hear in the movies.

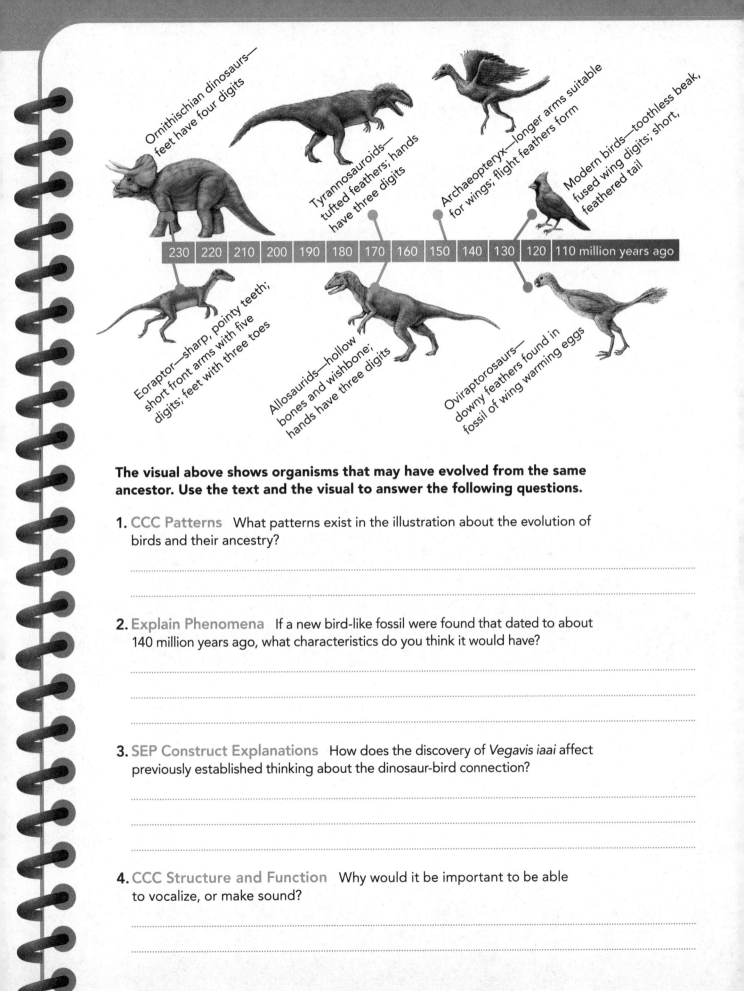

Ornithischian dinosaurs—
feet have four digits

Tyrannosauroids—
tufted feathers; hands
have three digits

Archaeopteryx—longer arms suitable
for wings; flight feathers form

Modern birds—toothless beak,
fused wing digits; short,
feathered tail

| 230 | 220 | 210 | 200 | 190 | 180 | 170 | 160 | 150 | 140 | 130 | 120 | 110 million years ago |

Eoraptor—sharp, pointy teeth;
short front arms with five
digits; feet with three toes

Allosaurids—hollow
bones and wishbone;
hands have three digits

Oviraptorosaurs—
downy feathers found in
fossil of wing warming eggs

The visual above shows organisms that may have evolved from the same ancestor. Use the text and the visual to answer the following questions.

1. **CCC Patterns**   What patterns exist in the illustration about the evolution of birds and their ancestry?

   ....

   ....

2. **Explain Phenomena**   If a new bird-like fossil were found that dated to about 140 million years ago, what characteristics do you think it would have?

   ....

   ....

   ....

3. **SEP Construct Explanations**   How does the discovery of *Vegavis iaai* affect previously established thinking about the dinosaur-bird connection?

   ....

   ....

   ....

4. **CCC Structure and Function**   Why would it be important to be able to vocalize, or make sound?

   ....

   ....

Other Evidence of Evolution

Guiding Questions

- How does modern technology provide evidence that all organisms have a common ancestor?
- What new discoveries about evolution has modern technology made possible?

Connections

Literacy Read and Comprehend

Math Use Algebraic Expressions

MS-LS4-2, MS-LS4-6

HANDS-ON LAB

uInvestigate Explore how DNA provides evidence for evolution.

Vocabulary

protein
endosymbiosis

Academic Vocabulary

transfer

Connect It!

✎ **Count the number of different kinds of organisms you see and write your number in the white circle on the photograph.**

SEP Engage in Argument from Evidence What do all the organisms in the photo have in common?

....

....

....

Using Technology to Study Evolution

Advances in technology have led to new knowledge about evolution. Darwin and scientists of his time used their eyes, hand tools, and simple microscopes to study evolution. Darwin's microscope had less than 200x magnification. Modern scientists have much better tools. We now have such powerful microscopes and imaging devices that computers can show us the shapes of individual molecules. Future advances may further our understanding of evolution.

Genetic Material and Evolution The coral reef in **Figure 1** contains an amazing variety of living things. The diverse shapes, body structures, and lifestyles are all due to differences in genetic material, the set of chemical instructions that guide the function and growth of an organism. Evolution results from changes in genetic material. Small changes in genetic material lead to microevolution within species. An accumulation of small changes causes macroevolution, or the creation of new species.

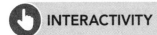

Literacy Connection

Read and Comprehend
As you work your way through this lesson, stop frequently to see if you understand what you just read. Each paragraph has key information. Try to restate it in your own words.

Rainbow of Life on a Reef
Figure 1 All of the differences among Earth's organisms result from evolutionary changes in genetic material.

Genetic Evidence for a Common Ancestor

Every living thing uses DNA for genetic material. Mosquitoes, humans, plants, and bacteria all have cells with the same system of genetic material. The shared use of DNA is one piece of evidence that every organism on Earth has a common ancestor. This common ancestor, called LUCA for Last Universal Common Ancestor, was most likely a single-celled organism similar to modern bacteria or archaea.

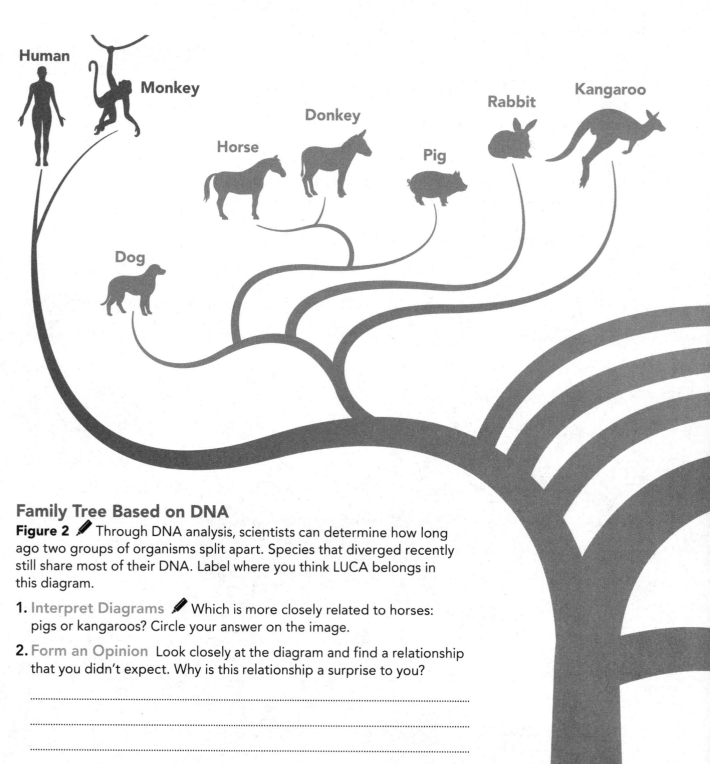

Family Tree Based on DNA

Figure 2 🖊 Through DNA analysis, scientists can determine how long ago two groups of organisms split apart. Species that diverged recently still share most of their DNA. Label where you think LUCA belongs in this diagram.

1. **Interpret Diagrams** 🖊 Which is more closely related to horses: pigs or kangaroos? Circle your answer on the image.

2. **Form an Opinion** Look closely at the diagram and find a relationship that you didn't expect. Why is this relationship a surprise to you?

....

....

....

Dawn of Evolution DNA is a complex molecule, difficult to copy without making any mistakes. LUCA started to change as it accumulated mutations, or changes to its DNA. Natural selection and other processes shaped LUCA's evolution. The original population of LUCA split and diverged, evolving into all the species that live or have ever lived on Earth. The traces of this evolution are recorded in the DNA of every organism. Shared DNA between species provides evidence of the evolutionary past. The more similar the DNA between two species, the more closely related they are. **Figure 2** shows a family tree based on differences in one stretch of DNA.

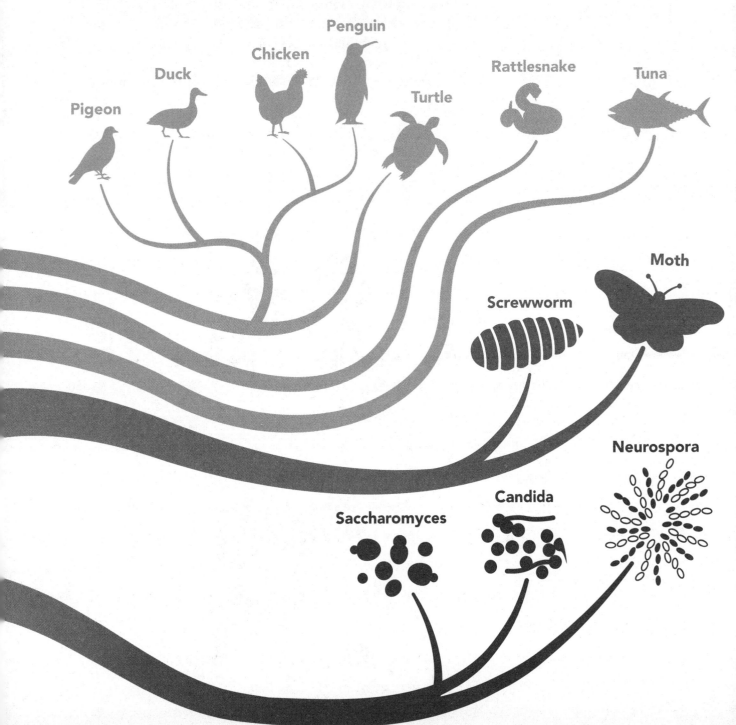

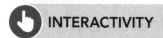

INTERACTIVITY

Explore how different types of evidence help to establish evolutionary relationships.

Proteins Recall that genes code for different **proteins**, which are complicated molecules that carry out important cellular functions. Proteins can act as the building blocks for cell materials and carry out important cellular functions. For example, some muscle fibers are made of chains of the protein actin. Other proteins act as messengers, fight diseases, carry out chemical reactions, or carry materials around the body.

Proteins and Evolution Consider what could happen to the function of a protein if the gene for it contains a mutation. The mutant genetic material may code for a different form of the protein, as shown in **Figure 3**. The new version of the protein may increase the individual's fitness. More likely, the mutation will lower the individual's fitness or leave it unchanged. Changes in proteins lead to variations within a population. Natural selection acts on those variations, causing evolution.

☑ READING CHECK **Determine Central Ideas** What are the possible effects of a mutation on the function of a protein?

....

....

Mutations and Proteins

Figure 3 The Mre11-Rad50 protein group helps cells to repair breaks in DNA molecules. There is only a small mutation in the genetic code for the bottom form.

Determine Differences How are the two forms of the protein group different?

....

....

....

....

....

....

....

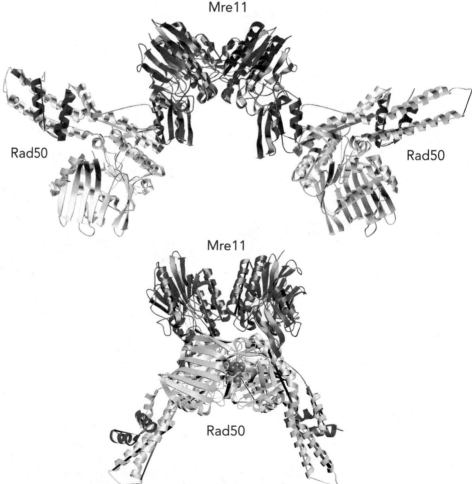

Mre11

Rad50   Rad50

Mre11

Rad50

Protein Analysis and Evolution Scientists compare proteins to see how closely any two species are related. In most cases, evidence from DNA and protein structure confirms conclusions based on fossils, embryos, and body structure. For example, DNA comparisons show that dogs are more similar to wolves than to coyotes. This confirms an earlier conclusion based on similarities in the structure and development of the three species.

Math Toolbox

All in the Family

Humans, apes, and monkeys are all members of the order Primates. Bonobos, chimpanzees, gorillas, and orangutans are all considered apes, but monkeys are not. Humans and monkeys share about 93 percent of their DNA.

Primate	Genetic Difference with Humans
Bonobo	1.2%
Chimpanzee	1.3%
Gorilla	1.6%
Orangutan	3.1%
Monkey	7.0%

1. **SEP Use Algebraic Expressions** Write an expression representing the percentage of DNA that gorillas share with humans. Let g = gorilla.

....

....

2. **Draw Comparative Inferences** What can you say about the evolutionary relationship between the apes and monkeys compared to humans?

....

....

An Evolutionary Leap

Figure 4 Normally, a new trait evolves over thousands of generations. In this case, bacteria species 2 gets a fully formed gene from a different species.

1. **Identify** 🖊 Label the transferred gene in Species 2.

2. **Predict** Will the transferred gene be passed on to the next generation? Explain.

....
....
....
....

Academic Vocabulary

You transfer your books from your locker into your school bag. How does this example help you understand what gene transfer is?

....
....
....
....

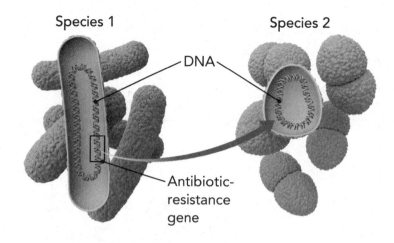

Species 1 | Species 2

DNA

Antibiotic-resistance gene

Gene Transfer Between Species

Individuals usually inherit DNA from their parent or parents. Surprisingly, scientists have discovered that genes can also pass between individuals from different species! The **transfer** of genes can happen when one cell engulfs another or when bacteria share their DNA with other cells. The transferred DNA is almost always destroyed. But occasionally, a cell adds the new genes to its DNA.

Bacteria use gene transfer to pass on adaptive traits. **Figure 4** shows how one bacterium can pass the trait of antibiotic resistance to a different species of bacteria. Being immune to antibiotics could provide a big boost for the bacterium in fitness for the bacterium. DNA analysis shows scientists which genes have passed from one species to another.

Designer Genes

By transferring helpful genes from one species directly into cells of another species, scientists can produce desired traits in an organism. This creates genetically modified organisms, or GMOs. Scientists have modified eggplant genes to produce an insect-resistant plant. Insects attacked the plants on the left, but not those that were modified on the right.

SEP Design a Solution 🖊 Draw an organism that you think could benefit from gene transfer and modification to become the next GMO. Label its features and describe the benefits.

Symbiosis Two organisms of different species that have a close relationship that involves living with each other is called symbiosis. In **endosymbiosis**, shown in **Figure 5**, one organism actually moves inside the other organism's cell. Scientists have theorized that endosymbiosis may be the mechanism that allowed life to generate on Earth. Mitochondria (the cell's power house) and chloroplasts (they capture the sun's energy and store it as food) are both organelles. Just as a bacterium cell contains its own DNA and ribosomes, so do mitochondria and chloroplasts. Bacteria, mitochondria, and chloroplasts are also similar in size. Over millions of years of evolution, one type of bacteria became mitochondria and another type of bacteria became chloroplasts. At first, many scientists rejected the idea that mitochondria and chloroplasts had evolved from bacteria. Finally, advances in technology led to DNA sequencing that gave evidence supporting the hypothesis.

✅ READING CHECK **Read and Comprehend** What are two ways that genetic material can move from one species to another?

....

....

Endosymbiosis
Figure 5 Evidence supports the idea that both mitochondria and chloroplasts evolved through endosymbiosis.

1. Integrate with Visuals
   ✏️ Label what happens in the two missing steps.

2. CCC Structure and Function Chloroplasts are parts of plant cells that turn sunlight into chemical energy for food. Consider how bacteria became chloroplasts. How might the bacteria have benefited from the arrangement?

....

....

1 There are two different bacteria cells.

2 ....
....

3 Now the larger cell has the smaller one living inside it.

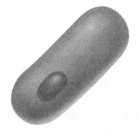

4 Both bacteria cells benefit.

5 ....
....

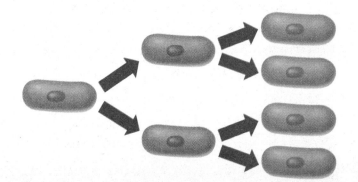

MS-LS4-2, MS-LS4-6

1. SEP Provide Evidence What evidence is there that every organism on Earth once had a common ancestor?

....

....

2. Compare and Contrast What do microevolution and macroevolution have in common? How do they differ?

....

....

....

....

3. Synthesize Information How have advances in technology supported the theory of evolution?

....

....

....

....

....

4. SEP Use Mathematics Refer to the data table in the Math Toolbox. Given that natural selection acts on variations and influences evolution, which two primate groups would you expect to have the most traits in common? Support your answer with a mathematical expression.

....

....

....

....

5. Support Your Explanation What does LUCA stand for and how did it evolve into all the life forms we see today?

....

....

....

....

....

....

....

....

Quest CHECK-IN

In this lesson, you learned more about how genetics drives evolution and how mutations to proteins lead to variations within a population.

CCC Cause and Effect What caused changes to the blackcap populations? How was natural selection at work here?

....

....

....

....

☝ INTERACTIVITY

Prepare Your Report

Go online to investigate the European blackcaps. Look for new information to add to your report. Brainstorm ideas for different ways to represent information.

MS-LS4-2, MS-LS4-4, MS-LS4-5

DNA, Fossils, and Evolution

All living things contain DNA. This blueprint carries the codes for every trait an organism expresses. We now have the technology to extract DNA from living things, as well as fossils, and then map out the locations of all the genes. By comparing modern DNA with that of fossils, it is possible to determine which traits similar species have in common.

Scientists are able to remove and analyze DNA from fossils using a process called an assay. DNA is removed from the center of a fossil and then prepared using an assortment of different chemicals. The DNA sample is then amplified and run through a process called gel electrophoresis. This separates different pieces of the DNA. The results are then compared to known DNA to see how similar they are.

One of the interesting things DNA research has discovered is that the domestication of dogs has changed their diet. While ancestral wolves ate mostly meat, modern dogs have more genes to help them digest starch and other carbohydrates. This suggests that the early dogs who could handle the starches in the human diet had an advantage.

MY DISCOVERY

With a classmate, research how dogs were domesticated from wolves. Engage in a classroom debate about the evidence that supports and refutes the descent of dogs from wolves.

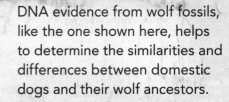

DNA evidence from wolf fossils, like the one shown here, helps to determine the similarities and differences between domestic dogs and their wolf ancestors.

121

☑ TOPIC 2 Review and Assess

1 Early Study of Evolution

MS-LS4-4

1. Adaptations and variations show evidence of past
   A. evolution.
   B. offspring.
   C. diversity.
   D. fossils.

2. Who made the first attempt at developing a theory of evolution?
   A. Anning
   B. Darwin
   C. Lamarck
   D. Lyell

3. On his five-year journey sailing around the world, Darwin was amazed by the .... of living things that he saw.

4. A species is a group of similar ....that can mate with each other and produce offspring capable of ....

5. **SEP Construct Explanations** Consider what caused the variation in finch beaks on the Galápagos Islands. How did it bring about new species of birds?

....

....

....

....

....

....

....

....

....

2 Natural Selection

MS-LS4-4, MS-LS4-5, MS-LS4-6

6. Darwin was able to create the fantail pigeon from the wild rock dove by using
   A. artificial selection.
   B. mechanisms.
   C. natural selection.
   D. overproduction.

7. Darwin observed that some variations make individuals better adapted
   A. to accumulate traits.
   B. to their environment.
   C. for population change.
   D. for more mutations.

8. Helpful variations may .... in a population, while unfavorable ones may disappear.

9. Natural selection is affected by three factors: ...., variations among members of the population, and

....

10. **Explain Phenomenon** How do environmental factors contribute to evolution by natural selection?

....

....

....

....

....

....

....

....

....

....

....

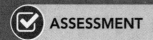
3 The Process of Evolution

MS-LS4-4, MS-LS4-6

11. Unlike an organism with low fitness, an organism with high fitness has the ability to survive and
   A. mutate.
   B. coevolve.
   C. reproduce.
   D. interact.

12. Because they create multiple alleles, mutations can cause
   A. cell division.
   B. damaged DNA to repair itself.
   C. overproduction of offspring.
   D. variations in traits.

13. ...., a mechanism of evolution, is a random, directionless process.

14. Mutations can occur when an organism is exposed to ....or certain chemicals that damage the cell's ....

15. Distinguish Relationships Consider two species that compete for the same resources. Might their interactions affect each other's evolution? Explain.

....
....
....
....
....
....
....
....

4 Evidence in the Fossil Record

MS-LS4-1, MS-LS4-2, MS-LS4-3, MS-LS4-6

16. Evidence supporting biological evolution is found in the fossil record and in
   A. adaptations to changing environments.
   B. similar anatomies and embryos.
   C. offspring with various traits.
   D. layers of sediment.

17. Support Your Explanations
What can you infer about this fossilized organism and its environment?

....
....
....
....
....
....
....

5 Other Evidence of Evolution

MS-LS4-2, MS-LS4-6

18. Evolution results from changes in
   A. genetic material.   B. migration patterns.
   C. habitats and climate.   D. the fossil record.

19. Apply Scientific Reasoning DNA comparisons show that dogs are more similar to wolves than to coyotes. How else could scientists confirm their close relationship?

....
....
....

MS-LS4-1, MS-LS4-4,
MS-LS4-6

Evidence-Based Assessment

A group of scientists was researching evolutionary relationships. They decided to investigate a particular protein called cytochrome-c. They compared the amino acid sequence that codes for the protein among several species. They made a surprising discovery. In moths, whales, and Baker's yeast—organisms that do not look at all related—almost half of the positions in the cytochrome-c amino acid sequence were identical.

Cytochrome-c is a very important protein when it comes to releasing energy from food. Like other proteins, cytochrome-c is made of a sequence of amino acids that may or may not vary among organisms. The analysis of cytochrome-c in different organisms provides strong evidence for determining which organisms are closely related. Scientists can predict evolutionary relationships by looking at the amino acid sequences in cytochrome-c that different organisms have in common.

The data table shows ten positions where there are different amino acids in the sequence that codes for the cytochrome-c protein from five different species. In all other positions, the amino acids are the same.

Species	Amino Acid, Position Number in Sequence									
	20	23	52	55	66	68	70	91	97	100
human	M	S	P	S	I	G	D	V	E	A
horse	Q	A	P	S	T	L	E	A	T	E
kangaroo	Q	A	P	T	I	G	D	A	G	A
pig	Q	A	P	S	T	G	E	A	G	E
whale	Q	A	V	S	T	G	E	A	G	A

SOURCE: National Center for Biotechnology Information

Amino Acid Symbols

A = Alanine   M = Methionine

D = Aspartic Acid   P = Proline

E = Glutamic Acid   Q = Glutamine

G = Glycine   S = Serine

I = Isoleucine   T = Threonine

L = Lysine   V = Valine

1. **SEP Analyze Data** According to cytochrome-c analysis, to which other species is the pig most closely related?
   A. human   **B.** horse
   C. kangaroo   **D.** whale

2. **Support Your Explanation** How did you determine the pig's closest relation among the four species? Use evidence from the data table to support your claim.

....

....

....

....

....

....

....

....

....

....

....

....

....

3. **SEP Cite Evidence** According to cytochrome-c analysis, which organism is least like the others? Cite evidence to support your claim.

....

....

....

....

....

....

....

....

4. **SEP Construct Arguments** Cows and sheep have the same sequence of amino acids in their cytochrome-c protein. How is it possible that they can be different species?

....

....

....

....

....

....

....

....

....

Quest FINDINGS

Complete the Quest!

Phenomenon Create a multimedia report about the two populations of European blackcaps and what caused them to be so different from each other.

Draw Conclusions If evolution continues, what can be said about the common ancestry of both populations of European blackcaps?

....

....

....

▶ **INTERACTIVITY**

Reflect on Blackcap Migration

MS-LS4-2, MS-LS4-4

A Bony Puzzle

How can you analyze **patterns** in structures to **show** evolutionary **relationships?**

Background

Phenomenon A new museum of natural history is opening in your community. The director of the museum has asked your class to help with an exhibit about evolutionary history. The director hopes you can show how patterns in skeletons provide clues about common ancestors.

In this investigation, you will analyze and compare the internal and external structures of a pigeon, a bat, and a rabbit. Then you will use the similarities and differences you observe to describe a possible common ancestor and infer evolutionary relationships among these organisms.

Materials

(per group)
- Activity Sheets 1, 2, and 3
- ruler

Eastern cottontail rabbit (*Sylvilagus floridanus*)

Rock pigeon (*Columba livia*)

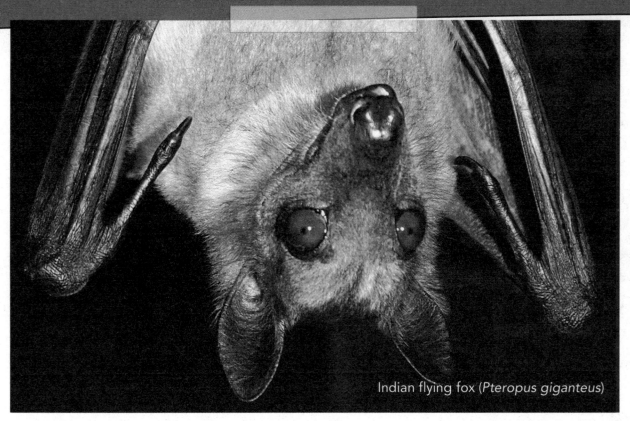

Indian flying fox (*Pteropus giganteus*)

Plan Your Investigation

1. Using the photographs and the diagrams, you will compare the features and structures of the pigeon, bat, and rabbit. You will look for patterns in the skeletons and note similarities and differences among the three animals.

2. Work with your group to plan a procedure for comparing the skeletons of the three animals. Write out your plan in the space provided. Consider the following questions as a guide for planning your procedure:

   - Should we compare all the bones shown in the diagrams or select a few important features that they all have in common to compare?

   - Do we also want to include our observations from the photographs of the animals?

   - What's the best way to record and organize our observations so we can analyze them more easily? Should we write notes summarizing what we see? Or should we use only data tables to organize the data?

3. After receiving your teacher's approval, follow the procedure your group developed. Remember that you may need to revise the plan as you carry it out. Record your observations about the three skeletons in the data tables.

HANDS-ON LAB

Demonstrate Go online for a downloadable worksheet of this lab.

Procedure

Observations

Skeleton	Similarities	Differences
Spine		
Skull		
Limbs		

Photos	Similarities	Differences
covering		
faces		
other		

Analyze and Interpret Data

1. **CCC Identify Patterns** What evidence did you find that will help you describe how these three skeletons are alike?

   ....

   ....

   ....

   ....

2. **SEP Evaluate Evidence** How does the skeleton pattern that you identified provide evidence for a common ancestor among the pigeon, bat, and rabbit?

   ....

   ....

   ....

3. **Explain Phenomena** Which bones of the common ancestor do you think might have changed the most in its descendants? Which bones remained about the same? Cite evidence from the skeleton diagrams to support your answer.

   ....

   ....

   ....

   ....

4. **CCC Structure and Function** How are the wings of the bat and the bird, and the rabbit's front legs, all examples of homologous structures? Use evidence from your investigation to support your answer.

   ....

   ....

   ....

   ....

5. **SEP Construct Explanations** The museum exhibit will include information to explain evolutionary relationships. What evidence can you use to show that bats share a more recent common ancestor with rabbits than they do with birds?

   ....

   ....

   ....

SEP.1, SEP.8

The Meaning of Science

Science Skills

Science is a way of learning about the natural world. It involves asking questions, making predictions, and collecting information to see if the answer is right or wrong.

The table lists some of the skills that scientists use. You use some of these skills every day. For example, you may observe and evaluate your lunch options before choosing what to eat.

Reflect Think about a time you misplaced something and could not find it. Write a sentence defining the problem. What science skills could you use to solve the problem? Explain how you would use at least three of the skills in the table.

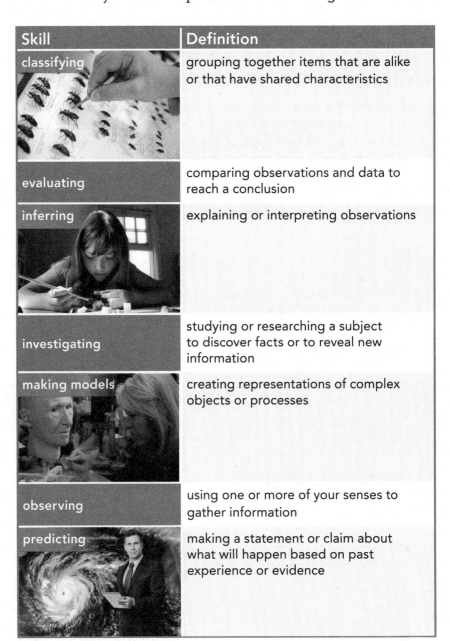

Skill	Definition
classifying	grouping together items that are alike or that have shared characteristics
evaluating	comparing observations and data to reach a conclusion
inferring	explaining or interpreting observations
investigating	studying or researching a subject to discover facts or to reveal new information
making models	creating representations of complex objects or processes
observing	using one or more of your senses to gather information
predicting	making a statement or claim about what will happen based on past experience or evidence

Scientific Attitudes

Curiosity often drives scientists to learn about the world around them. Creativity is useful for coming up with inventive ways to solve problems. Such qualities and attitudes, and the ability to keep an open mind, are essential for scientists.

When sharing results or findings, honesty and ethics are also essential. Ethics refers to rules for knowing right from wrong.

Being skeptical is also important. This means having doubts about things based on past experiences and evidence. Skepticism helps to prevent accepting data and results that may not be true.

Scientists must also avoid bias—likes or dislikes of people, ideas, or things. They must avoid experimental bias, which is a mistake that may make an experiment's preferred outcome more likely.

Scientific Reasoning

Scientific reasoning depends on being logical and objective. When you are objective, you use evidence and apply logic to draw conclusions. Being subjective means basing conclusions on personal feelings, biases, or opinions. Subjective reasoning can interfere with science and skew results. Objective reasoning helps scientists use observations to reach conclusions about the natural world.

Scientists use two types of objective reasoning: deductive and inductive. Deductive reasoning involves starting with a general idea or theory and applying it to a situation. For example, the theory of plate tectonics indicates that earthquakes happen mostly where tectonic plates meet. You could then draw the conclusion, or deduce, that California has many earthquakes because tectonic plates meet there.

In inductive reasoning, you make a generalization from a specific observation. When scientists collect data in an experiment and draw a conclusion based on that data, they use inductive reasoning. For example, if fertilizer causes one set of plants to grow faster than another, you might infer that the fertilizer promotes plant growth.

Make Meaning
Think about a bias the marine biologist in the photo could show that results in paying more or less attention to one kind of organism over others. Make a prediction about how that bias could affect the biologist's survey of the coral reef.

Write About It
Suppose it is raining when you go to sleep one night. When you wake up the next morning, you observe frozen puddles on the ground and icicles on tree branches. Use scientific reasoning to draw a conclusion about the air temperature outside. Support your conclusion using deductive or inductive reasoning.

SEP.1, SEP.2, SEP.3, SEP.4, CCC.4

Science Processes

Scientific Inquiry

Scientists contribute to scientific knowledge by conducting investigations and drawing conclusions. The process often begins with an observation that leads to a question, which is then followed by the development of a hypothesis. This is known as scientific inquiry.

One of the first steps in scientific inquiry is asking questions. However, it's important to make a question specific with a narrow focus so the investigation will not be too broad. A biologist may want to know all there is to know about wolves, for example. But a good, focused question for a specific inquiry might be "How many offspring does the average female wolf produce in her lifetime?"

A hypothesis is a possible answer to a scientific question. A hypothesis must be testable. For something to be testable, researchers must be able to carry out an investigation and gather evidence that will either support or disprove the hypothesis.

Scientific Models

Models are tools that scientists use to study phenomena indirectly. A model is any representation of an object or process. Illustrations, dioramas, globes, diagrams, computer programs, and mathematical equations are all examples of scientific models. For example, a diagram of Earth's crust and mantle can help you to picture layers deep below the surface and understand events such as volcanic eruptions.

📓 **Reflect** Identify the benefits and limitations of using a plastic model of DNA, as shown here.

Models also allow scientists to represent objects that are either very large, such as our solar system, or very small, such as a molecule of DNA. Models can also represent processes that occur over a long period of time, such as the changes that have occurred throughout Earth's history.

Models are helpful, but they have limitations. Physical models are not made of the same materials as the objects they represent. Most models of complex objects or processes show only major parts, stages, or relationships. Many details are left out. Therefore, you may not be able to learn as much from models as you would through direct observation.

Science Experiments

An experiment or investigation must be well planned to produce valid results. In planning an experiment, you must identify the independent and dependent variables. You must also do as much as possible to remove the effects of other variables. A controlled experiment is one in which you test only one variable at a time.

For example, suppose you plan a controlled experiment to learn how the type of material affects the speed at which sound waves travel through it. The only variable that should change is the type of material. This way, if the speed of sound changes, you know that it is a result of a change in the material, not another variable such as the thickness of the material or the type of sound used.

You should also remove bias from any investigation. You may inadvertently introduce bias by selecting subjects you like and avoiding those you don't like. Scientists often conduct investigations by taking random samples to avoid ending up with biased results.

Once you plan your investigation and begin to collect data, it's important to record and organize the data. You may wish to use a graph to display and help you to interpret the data.

Communicating is the sharing of ideas and results with others through writing and speaking. Communicating data and conclusions is a central part of science.

Scientists share knowledge, including new findings, theories, and techniques for collecting data. Conferences, journals, and websites help scientists to communicate with each other. Popular media, including newspapers, magazines, and social media sites, help scientists to share their knowledge with nonscientists. However, before the results of investigations are shared and published, other scientists should review the experiment for possible sources of error, such as bias and unsupported conclusions.

Write About It
List four ways you could communicate the results of a scientific study about the health of sea turtles in the Pacific Ocean.

SEP.1, SEP.6, SEP.7, SEP.8

Scientific Knowledge

Scientific Explanations

Suppose you learn that adult flamingos are pink because of the food they eat. This statement is a scientific explanation—it describes how something in nature works or explains why it happens. Scientists from different fields use methods such as researching information, designing experiments, and making models to form scientific explanations. Scientific explanations often result from many years of work and multiple investigations conducted by many scientists.

Scientific Theories and Laws

A scientific law is a statement that describes what you can expect to occur every time under a particular set of conditions. A scientific law describes an observed pattern in nature, but it does not attempt to explain it. For example, the law of superposition describes what you can expect to find in terms of the ages of layers of rock. Geologists use this observed pattern to determine the relative ages of sedimentary rock layers. But the law does not explain why the pattern occurs.

By contrast, a scientific theory is a well-tested explanation for a wide range of observations or experimental results. It provides details and describes causes of observed patterns. Something is elevated to a theory only when there is a large body of evidence that supports it. However, a scientific theory can be changed or overturned when new evidence is found.

✐ Write About It
Choose two fields of science that interest you. Describe a method used to develop scientific explanations in each field.

SEP Construct Explanations Complete the table to compare and contrast a scientific theory and a scientific law.

	Scientific Theory	Scientific Law
Definition		
Does it attempt to explain a pattern observed in nature?		

Analyzing Scientific Explanations

To analyze scientific explanations that you hear on the news or read in a book such as this one, you need scientific literacy. Scientific literacy means understanding scientific terms and principles well enough to ask questions, evaluate information, and make decisions. Scientific reasoning gives you a process to apply. This includes looking for bias and errors in the research, evaluating data, and identifying faulty reasoning. For example, by evaluating how a survey was conducted, you may find a serious flaw in the researchers' methods.

Evidence and Opinions

The basis for scientific explanations is empirical evidence. Empirical evidence includes the data and observations that have been collected through scientific processes. Satellite images, photos, and maps of mountains and volcanoes are all examples of empirical evidence that support a scientific explanation about Earth's tectonic plates. Scientists look for patterns when they analyze this evidence. For example, they might see a pattern that mountains and volcanoes often occur near tectonic plate boundaries.

To evaluate scientific information, you must first distinguish between evidence and opinion. In science, evidence includes objective observations and conclusions that have been repeated. Evidence may or may not support a scientific claim. An opinion is a subjective idea that is formed from evidence, but it cannot be confirmed by evidence.

Write About It
Suppose the conservation committee of a town wants to gauge residents' opinions about a proposal to stock the local ponds with fish every spring. The committee pays for a survey to appear on a web site that is popular with people who like to fish. The results of the survey show 78 people in favor of the proposal and two against it. Do you think the survey's results are valid? Explain.

Make Meaning
Explain what empirical evidence the photograph reveals.

SEP.3, SEP.4

Tools of Science

Measurement

Making measurements using standard units is important in all fields of science. This allows scientists to repeat and reproduce other experiments, as well as to understand the precise meaning of the results of others. Scientists use a measurement system called the International System of Units, or SI.

For each type of measurement, there is a series of units that are greater or less than each other. The unit a scientist uses depends on what is being measured. For example, a geophysicist tracking the movements of tectonic plates may use centimeters, as plates tend to move small amounts each year. Meanwhile, a marine biologist might measure the movement of migrating bluefin tuna on the scale of kilometers.

Units for length, mass, volume, and density are based on powers of ten—a meter is equal to 100 centimeters or 1000 millimeters. Units of time do not follow that pattern. There are 60 seconds in a minute, 60 minutes in an hour, and 24 hours in a day. These units are based on patterns that humans perceived in nature. Units of temperature are based on scales that are set according to observations of nature. For example, 0°C is the temperature at which pure water freezes, and 100°C is the temperature at which it boils.

Write About It

Suppose you are planning an investigation in which you must measure the dimensions of several small mineral samples that fit in your hand. Which metric unit or units will you most likely use? Explain your answer.

Measurement	Metric units
Length or distance	meter (m), kilometer (km), centimeter (cm), millimeter (mm) 1 km = 1,000 m 1 cm = 10 mm 1 m = 100 cm
Mass	kilogram (kg), gram (g), milligram (mg) 1 kg = 1,000 g 1 g = 1,000 mg
Volume	cubic meter (m^3), cubic centimeter (cm^3) 1 m^3 = 1,000,000 cm^3
Density	kilogram per cubic meter (kg/m^3), gram per cubic centimeter (g/cm^3) 1,000 kg/m^3 = 1 g/cm^3
Temperature	degrees Celsius (°C), kelvin (K) 1°C = 273 K
Time	hour (h), minute (m), second (s)

Math Skills

Using numbers to collect and interpret data involves math skills that are essential in science. For example, you use math skills when you estimate the number of birds in an entire forest after counting the actual number of birds in ten trees.

Scientists evaluate measurements and estimates for their precision and accuracy. In science, an accurate measurement is very close to the actual value. Precise measurements are very close, or nearly equal, to each other. Reliable measurements are both accurate and precise. An imprecise value may be a sign of an error in data collection. This kind of anomalous data may be excluded to avoid skewing the data and harming the investigation.

Other math skills include performing specific calculations, such as finding the mean, or average, value in a data set. The mean can be calculated by adding up all of the values in the data set and then dividing that sum by the number of values.

Hour	Number of Ducks Observed at a Pond
1	12
2	10
3	2
4	14
5	13
6	10
7	11

SEP Use Mathematics The data table shows how many ducks were seen at a pond every hour over the course of seven hours. Is there a data point that seems anomalous? If so, cross out that data point. Then, calculate the mean number of ducks on the pond. Round the mean to the nearest whole number.

Graphs

Graphs help scientists to interpret data by helping them to find trends or patterns in the data. A line graph displays data that show how one variable (the dependent or outcome variable) changes in response to another (the independent or test variable). The slope and shape of a graph line can reveal patterns and help scientists to make predictions. For example, line graphs can help you to spot patterns of change over time.

Scientists use bar graphs to compare data across categories or subjects that may not affect each other. The heights of the bars make it easy to compare those quantities. A circle graph, also known as a pie chart, shows the proportions of different parts of a whole.

Write About It
You and a friend record the distance you travel every 15 minutes on a one-hour bike trip. Your friend wants to display the data as a circle graph. Explain whether or not this is the best type of graph to display your data. If not, suggest another graph to use.

SEP.1, SEP.2, SEP.3, SEP.6

The Engineering Design Process

Engineers are builders and problem solvers. Chemical engineers experiment with new fuels made from algae. Civil engineers design roadways and bridges. Bioengineers develop medical devices and prosthetics. The common trait among engineers is an ability to identify problems and design solutions to solve them. Engineers use a creative process that relies on scientific methods to help guide them from a concept or idea all the way to the final product.

Define the Problem

To identify or define a problem, different questions need to be asked: *What are the effects of the problem? What are the likely causes? What other factors could be involved?* Sometimes the obvious, immediate cause of a problem may be the result of another problem that may not be immediately apparent. For example, climate change results in different weather patterns, which in turn can affect organisms that live in certain habitats. So engineers must be aware of all the possible effects of potential solutions. Engineers must also take into account how well different solutions deal with the different causes of the problem.

Reflect Write about a problem that you encountered in your life that had both immediate, obvious causes as well as less-obvious and less-immediate ones.

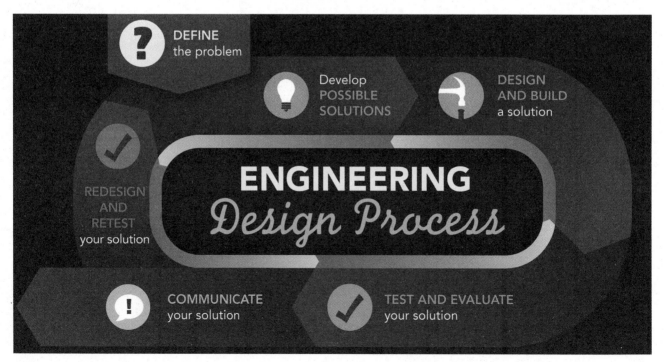

DEFINE the problem

Develop POSSIBLE SOLUTIONS

DESIGN AND BUILD a solution

REDESIGN AND RETEST your solution

ENGINEERING *Design Process*

COMMUNICATE your solution

TEST AND EVALUATE your solution

As engineers consider problems and design solutions, they must identify and categorize the criteria and constraints of the project.

Criteria are the factors that must be met or accomplished by the solution. For example, a gardener who wants to protect outdoor plants from deer and rabbits may say that the criteria for the solution are "plants are no longer eaten" and "plant growth is not inhibited in any way." The gardener then knows the plants cannot simply be sealed off from the environment, because the plants will not receive sunlight and water.

The same gardener will likely have constraints on his solution, such as budget for materials and time that is available for working on the project. By setting constraints, a solution can be designed that will be successful without introducing a new set of problems. No one wants to spend $500 on materials to protect $100 worth of tomatoes and cucumbers.

Develop Possible Solutions

After the problem has been identified, and the criteria and constraints identified, an engineer will consider possible solutions. This often involves working in teams with other engineers and designers to brainstorm ideas and research materials that can be used in the design.

It's important for engineers to think creatively and explore all potential solutions. If you wanted to design a bicycle that was safer and easier to ride than a traditional bicycle, then you would want more than just one or two solutions. Having multiple ideas to choose from increases the likelihood that you will develop a solution that meets the criteria and constraints. In addition, different ideas that result from brainstorming can often lead to new and better solutions to an existing problem.

Make Meaning

Using the example of a garden that is vulnerable to wild animals such as deer, make a list of likely constraints on an engineering solution to the problem you identified before. Determine if there are common traits among the constraints, and identify categories for them.

Design a Solution

Engineers then develop the idea that they feel best solves the problem. Once a solution has been chosen, engineers and designers get to work building a model or prototype of the solution. A model may involve sketching on paper or using computer software to construct a model of the solution. A prototype is a working model of the solution.

Building a model or prototype helps an engineer determine whether a solution meets the criteria and stays within the constraints. During this stage of the process, engineers must often deal with new problems and make any necessary adjustments to the model or prototype.

Test and Evaluate a Solution

Whether testing a model or a prototype, engineers use scientific processes to evaluate their solutions. Multiple experiments, tests, or trials are conducted, data are evaluated, and results and analyses are communicated. New criteria or constraints may emerge as a result of testing. In most cases, a solution will require some refinement or revision, even if it has been through successful testing. Refining a solution is necessary if there are new constraints, such as less money or available materials. Additional testing may be done to ensure that a solution satisfies local, state, or federal laws or standards.

Make Meaning Think about an aluminum beverage can. What would happen if the price or availability of aluminum changed so much that cans needed to be made of a new material? What would the criteria and constraints be on the development of a new can?

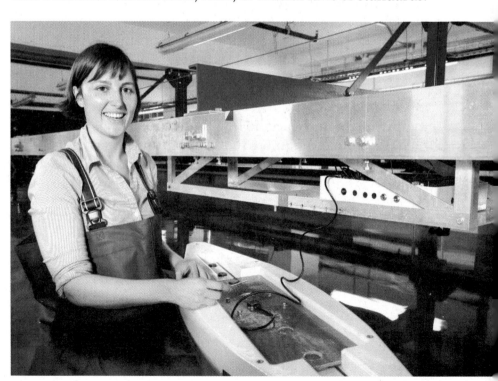

A naval architect sets up a model to test how the the hull's design responds to waves.

Communicate the Solution

Engineers need to communicate the final design to the people who will manufacture the product. This may include sketches, detailed drawings, computer simulations, and written text. Engineers often provide evidence that was collected during the testing stage. This evidence may include graphs and data tables that support the decisions made for the final design.

If there is feedback about the solution, then the engineers and designers must further refine the solution. This might involve making minor adjustments to the design, or it might mean bigger modifications to the design based on new criteria or constraints. Any changes in the design will require additional testing to make sure that the changes work as intended.

Redesign and Retest the Solution

At different steps in the engineering and design process, a solution usually must be revised and retested. Many designs fail to work perfectly, even after models and prototypes are built, tested, and evaluated. Engineers must be ready to analyze new results and deal with any new problems that arise. Troubleshooting, or fixing design problems, allows engineers to adjust the design to improve on how well the solution meets the need.

SEP Communicate Information Suppose you are an engineer at an aerospace company. Your team is designing a rover to be used on a future NASA space mission. A family member doesn't understand why so much of your team's time is taken up with testing and retesting the rover design. What are three things you would tell your relative to explain why testing and retesting are so important to the engineering and design process?

....

....

....

....

....

....

....

....

APPENDIX A

Safety Symbols

These symbols warn of possible dangers in the laboratory and remind you to work carefully.

 Safety Goggles Wear safety goggles to protect your eyes in any activity involving chemicals, flames or heating, or glassware.

 Lab Apron Wear a laboratory apron to protect your skin and clothing from damage.

 Breakage Handle breakable materials, such as glassware, with care. Do not touch broken glassware.

 Heat-Resistant Gloves Use an oven mitt or other hand protection when handling hot materials, such as hot plates or hot glassware.

 Plastic Gloves Wear disposable plastic gloves when working with harmful chemicals and organisms. Keep your hands away from your face, and dispose of the gloves according to your teacher's instructions.

 Heating Use a clamp or tongs to pick up hot glassware. Do not touch hot objects with your bare hands.

 Flames Before you work with flames, tie back loose hair and clothing. Follow your teacher's instructions about lighting and extinguishing flames.

 No Flames When using flammable materials, make sure there are no flames, sparks, or other exposed heat sources present.

 Corrosive Chemical Avoid getting acid or other corrosive chemicals on your skin or clothing or in your eyes. Do not inhale the vapors. Wash your hands after the activity.

 Poison Do not let any poisonous chemical come into contact with your skin, and do not inhale its vapors. Wash your hands when you are finished with the activity.

 Fumes Work in a well-ventilated area when harmful vapors may be involved. Avoid inhaling vapors directly. Test an odor only when directed to do so by your teacher, and use a wafting motion to direct the vapor toward your nose.

 Sharp Object Scissors, scalpels, knives, needles, pins, and tacks can cut your skin. Always direct a sharp edge or point away from yourself and others.

 Animal Safety Treat live or preserved animals or animal parts with care to avoid harming the animals or yourself. Wash your hands when you are finished with the activity.

 Plant Safety Handle plants only as directed by your teacher. If you are allergic to certain plants, tell your teacher; do not do an activity involving those plants. Avoid touching harmful plants such as poison ivy. Wash your hands when you are finished with the activity.

 Electric Shock To avoid electric shock, never use electrical equipment around water, when the equipment is wet, or when your hands are wet. Be sure cords are untangled and cannot trip anyone. Unplug equipment not in use.

 Physical Safety When an experiment involves physical activity, avoid injuring yourself or others. Alert your teacher if there is any reason you should not participate.

 Disposal Dispose of chemicals and other laboratory materials safely. Follow the instructions from your teacher.

 Hand Washing Wash your hands thoroughly when finished with an activity. Use soap and warm water. Rinse well.

 General Safety Awareness When this symbol appears, follow the instructions provided. When you are asked to develop your own procedure in a lab, have your teacher approve your plan.

Using a Laboratory Balance

The laboratory balance is an important tool in scientific investigations. Different kinds of balances are used in the laboratory to determine the masses and weights of objects. You can use a triple-beam balance to determine the masses of materials that you study or experiment with in the laboratory. An electronic balance, unlike a triple-beam balance, is used to measure the weights of materials.

The triple-beam balance that you may use in your science class is probably similar to the balance depicted in this Appendix. To use the balance properly, you should learn the name, location, and function of each part of the balance.

Triple-Beam Balance

The triple-beam balance is a single-pan balance with three beams calibrated in grams. The back, or 100-gram, beam is divided into ten units of 10 grams each. The middle, or 500-gram, beam is divided into five units of 100 grams each. The front, or 10-gram, beam is divided into ten units of 1 gram each. Each gram on the front beam is further divided into units of 0.1 gram.

Apply Concepts What is the greatest mass you could find with the triple-beam balance in the picture?

....

Calculate What is the mass of the apple in the picture?

....

The following procedure can be used to find the mass of an object with a triple-beam balance:

1. Place the object on the pan.

2. Move the rider on the middle beam notch by notch until the horizontal pointer on the right drops below zero. Move the rider back one notch.

3. Move the rider on the back beam notch by notch until the pointer again drops below zero. Move the rider back one notch.

4. Slowly slide the rider along the front beam until the pointer stops at the zero point.

5. The mass of the object is equal to the sum of the readings on the three beams.

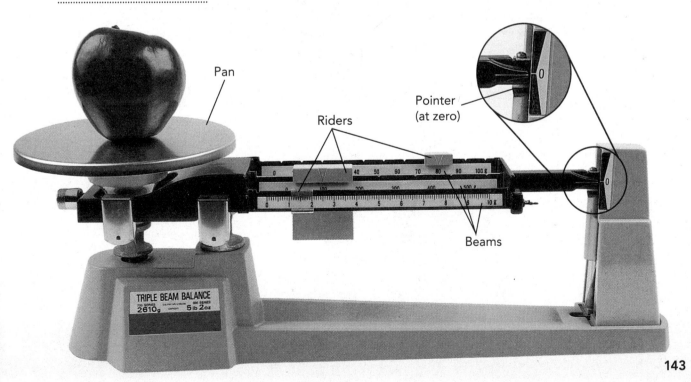

Pan

Riders

Pointer (at zero)

Beams

TRIPLE BEAM BALANCE
2610 g   5 lb 2 oz

Using a Microscope

The microscope is an essential tool in the study of life science. It allows you to see things that are too small to be seen with the unaided eye.

You will probably use a compound microscope like the one you see here. The compound microscope has more than one lens that magnifies the object you view.

Typically, a compound microscope has one lens in the eyepiece (the part you look through). The eyepiece lens usually magnifies 10×. Any object you view through this lens will appear 10 times larger than it is.

A compound microscope may contain two or three other lenses called objective lenses. They are called the low-power and high-power objective lenses. The low-power objective lens usually magnifies 10×. The high-power objective lenses usually magnify 40× and 100×.

To calculate the total magnification with which you are viewing an object, multiply the magnification of the eyepiece lens by the magnification of the objective lens you are using. For example, the eyepiece's magnification of 10× multiplied by the low-power objective's magnification of 10× equals a total magnification of 100×.

Use the photo of the compound microscope to become familiar with the parts of the microscope and their functions.

The Parts of a Microscope

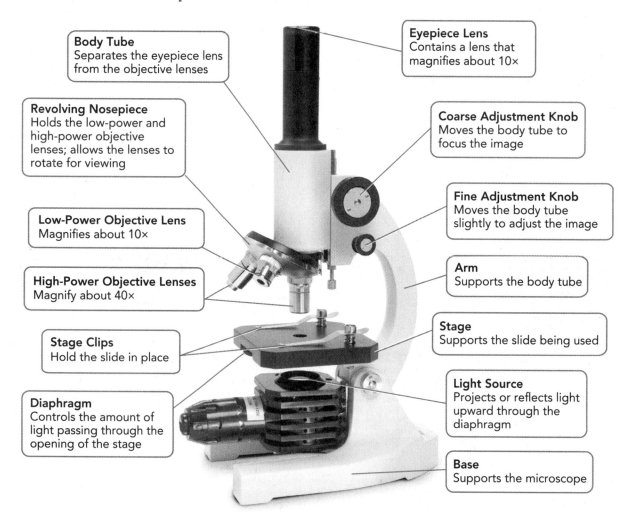

Body Tube
Separates the eyepiece lens from the objective lenses

Revolving Nosepiece
Holds the low-power and high-power objective lenses; allows the lenses to rotate for viewing

Low-Power Objective Lens
Magnifies about 10×

High-Power Objective Lenses
Magnify about 40×

Stage Clips
Hold the slide in place

Diaphragm
Controls the amount of light passing through the opening of the stage

Eyepiece Lens
Contains a lens that magnifies about 10×

Coarse Adjustment Knob
Moves the body tube to focus the image

Fine Adjustment Knob
Moves the body tube slightly to adjust the image

Arm
Supports the body tube

Stage
Supports the slide being used

Light Source
Projects or reflects light upward through the diaphragm

Base
Supports the microscope

Using the Microscope
Use the following procedures when you are working with a microscope.

1. To carry the microscope, grasp the microscope's arm with one hand. Place your other hand under the base.

2. Place the microscope on a table with the arm toward you.

3. Turn the coarse adjustment knob to raise the body tube.

4. Revolve the nosepiece until the low-power objective lens clicks into place.

5. Adjust the diaphragm. While looking through the eyepiece, adjust the mirror until you see a bright white circle of light. **CAUTION:** Never use direct sunlight as a light source.

6. Place a slide on the stage. Center the specimen over the opening on the stage. Use the stage clips to hold the slide in place. **CAUTION:** Glass slides are fragile.

7. Look at the stage from the side. Carefully turn the coarse adjustment knob to lower the body tube until the low-power objective almost touches the slide.

8. Looking through the eyepiece, very slowly turn the coarse adjustment knob until the specimen comes into focus.

9. To switch to the high-power objective lens, look at the microscope from the side. Carefully revolve the nosepiece until the high-power objective lens clicks into place. Make sure the lens does not hit the slide.

10. Looking through the eyepiece, turn the fine adjustment knob until the specimen comes into focus.

Making a Wet-Mount Slide
Use the following procedures to make a wet-mount slide of a specimen.

1. Obtain a clean microscope slide and a coverslip. **CAUTION:** Glass slides and coverslips are fragile.

2. Place the specimen on the center of the slide. The specimen must be thin enough for light to pass through it.

3. Using a plastic dropper, place a drop of water on the specimen.

4. Gently place one edge of the coverslip against the slide so that it touches the edge of the water drop at a 45° angle. Slowly lower the coverslip over the specimen. If you see air bubbles trapped beneath the coverslip, tap the coverslip gently with the eraser end of a pencil.

5. Remove any excess water at the edge of the coverslip with a paper towel.

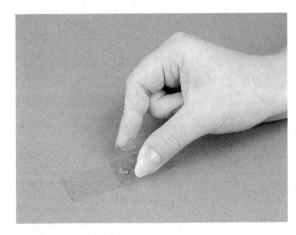

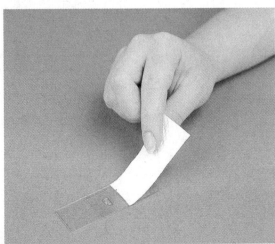

Periodic Table of Elements

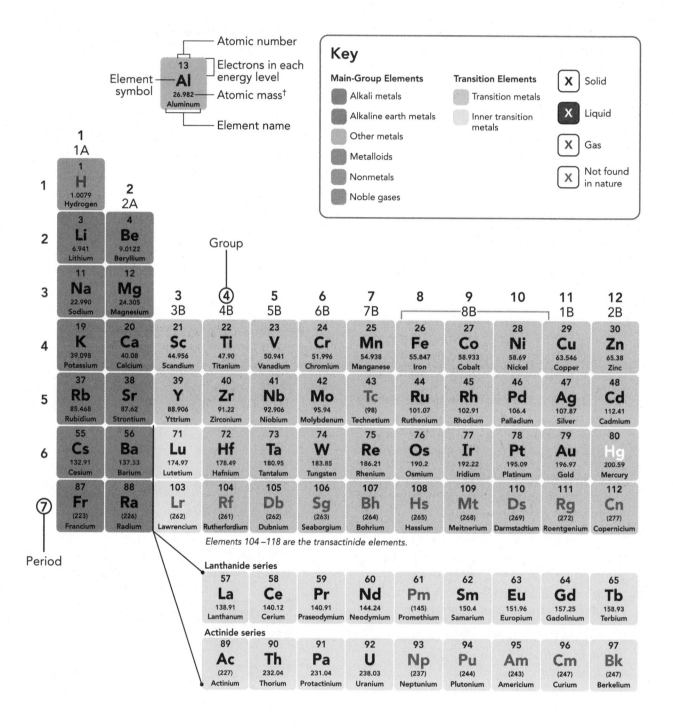

Elements 104–118 are the transactinide elements.

13 3A	14 4A	15 5A	16 6A	17 7A	18 8A
					2 **He** 4.0026 Helium
5 **B** 10.81 Boron	6 **C** 12.011 Carbon	7 **N** 14.007 Nitrogen	8 **O** 15.999 Oxygen	9 **F** 18.998 Fluorine	10 **Ne** 20.179 Neon
13 **Al** 26.982 Aluminum	14 **Si** 28.086 Silicon	15 **P** 30.974 Phosphorus	16 **S** 32.06 Sulfur	17 **Cl** 35.453 Chlorine	18 **Ar** 39.948 Argon
31 **Ga** 69.72 Gallium	32 **Ge** 72.59 Germanium	33 **As** 74.922 Arsenic	34 **Se** 78.96 Selenium	35 **Br** 79.904 Bromine	36 **Kr** 83.80 Krypton
49 **In** 114.82 Indium	50 **Sn** 118.69 Tin	51 **Sb** 121.75 Antimony	52 **Te** 127.60 Tellurium	53 **I** 126.90 Iodine	54 **Xe** 131.30 Xenon
81 **Tl** 204.37 Thallium	82 **Pb** 207.2 Lead	83 **Bi** 208.98 Bismuth	84 **Po** (209) Polonium	85 **At** (210) Astatine	86 **Rn** (222) Radon
113 **Nh** (284) Nihonium	114 **Fl** (289) Flerovium	115 **Mc** (288) Moscovium	116 **Lv** (292) Livermorium	117 **Ts** (294) Tennessine	118 **Og** (294) Oganesson

66 **Dy** 162.50 Dysprosium	67 **Ho** 164.93 Holmium	68 **Er** 167.26 Erbium	69 **Tm** 168.93 Thulium	70 **Yb** 173.04 Ytterbium
98 **Cf** (251) Californium	99 **Es** (252) Einsteinium	100 **Fm** (257) Fermium	101 **Md** (258) Mendelevium	102 **No** (259) Nobelium

GLOSSARY

A

adaptation An inherited behavior or physical characteristic that helps an organism survive and reproduce in its environment. (77)

artificial selection The process by which humans breed only those organisms with desired traits to produce the next generation; selective breeding. (49)

autosomal chromosomes The 22 pairs of chromosomes that are not sex chromosomes. (38)

C

cell cycle The series of events in which a cell grows, prepares for division, and divides to form two daughter cells. (17)

chromatid The structure formed when a chromosome divides during meiosis (22)

chromosome A threadlike structure within a cell's nucleus that contains DNA that is passed from one generation to the next. (17)

clone An organism that is genetically identical to the organism from which it was produced. (53)

coevolution The process by which two species evolve in response to changes in each other over time. (96)

competition The struggle between organisms to survive as they attempt to use the same limited resources in the same place at the same time. (83)

D

DNA Deoxyribonucleic acid; the genetic material that carries information about an organism and is passed from parent to offspring. (27)

dominant allele An allele whose trait always shows up in the organism when the allele is present. (7)

E

embryo The young organism that develops from a zygote. (104)

endosymbiosis A relationship in which one organism lives inside another organism's cells. (119)

evolution Change over time; the process by which modern organisms have descended from ancient organisms. (71)

extinct 1. Term used to describe a volcano that is no longer active and unlikely to erupt again. 2. Term used to refer to a group of related organisms that has died out and has no living members. (106)

F

fitness How well an organism can survive and reproduce in its environment. (91)

fossil The preserved remains or traces of an organism that lived in the past. (74)

fossil record All the fossils that have been discovered and what scientists have learned from them. (99)

G

gene therapy The process of replacing an absent or faulty gene with a normal working gene to treat a disease or medical disorder. (52)

genetic engineering The transfer of a gene from the DNA of one organism into another organism, in order to produce an organism with desired traits. (50)

genome The complete set of genetic information that an organism carries in its DNA. (54)

genotype An organism's genetic makeup, or allele combinations. (12)

H

heredity The passing of traits from parents to offspring. (5)

homologous structures Structures that are similar in different species and that have been inherited from a common ancestor. (104)

M

mechanism The natural process by which something takes place. (81)

meiosis The process that occurs in the formation of sex cells (sperm and egg) by which the number of chromosomes is reduced by half. (21)

messenger RNA Type of RNA that carries copies of instructions for the assembly of amino acids into proteins from DNA to ribosomes in the cytoplasm. (31)

mitosis The second stage of the cell cycle during which the cell's nucleus divides into two new nuclei and one set of DNA is distributed into each daughter cell. (23)

mutation Any change in the DNA of a gene or a chromosome. (40)

N

natural selection The process by which organisms that are best adapted to their environment are most likely to survive and reproduce. (83)

P

pedigree A tool that geneticists use to map out the inheritance of traits. (20)

phenotype An organism's physical appearance, or visible traits. (12)

probability A number that describes how likely it is that a particular event will occur. (9)

protein Large organic molecule made of carbon, hydrogen, oxygen, nitrogen, and sometimes sulfur. (116)

protein synthesis The process by which amino acids link together to form proteins. (30)

R

recessive allele An allele that is hidden whenever the dominant allele is present. (7)

S

scientific theory A well-tested explanation for a wide range of observations or experimental results. (78)

sex chromosomes The pair of chromosomes carrying genes that determine whether a person is biologically male or female. (38)

sex-linked gene A gene carried on a sex chromosome. (41)

sexual selection A type of natural selection that acts on an organism's ability to get the best possible mate. (95)

species A group of similar organisms that can mate with each other and produce offspring that can also mate and reproduce. (71)

T

transfer RNA Type of RNA in the cytoplasm that carries an amino acid to the ribosome during protein synthesis. (31)

V

variation Any difference between individuals of the same species. (37)

CREDITS

Photographs
Photo locators denoted as follows: Top (T), Center (C), Bottom (B), Left (L), Right (R), Background (Bkgd)

Covers
Front Cover: NatalieJean/Shutterstock
Back Cover: LHF Graphics/Shutterstock

Front Matter
iv: Clari Massimiliano/Shutterstock; vi: Buffy1982/Fotolia; vii: Tonyz20/Shutterstock; viii: Brian J. Skerry/National Geographic/Getty Images; ix: Gary Meszaros/Science Source/Getty Images;

Topic 1
x: Buffy1982/Fotolia; 003 Bkgrd: Tim Gainey/Alamy Stock Photo; 003 TR: Luis Abrantes/Shutterstock; 004: Svetlana Foote/Alamy Stock Photo; 008: Martin Shields/Alamy Stock Photo; 009: James Steidl/Shutterstock; 010: Martin Shields/Alamy Stock Photo; 014 Bkgd: Martin Strmiska/Alamy Stock Photo; 014 CL: Images & Stories/Alamy Stock Photo; 015: David Litman/Shutterstock; 016: Cuppyuppycake Creative/Getty Images; 025 BR: MixAll Studio Creative/Getty Images; 025 TR: Miodrag Gajic/Getty Images; 027: UpperCut Images/Alamy Stock Photo; 035: Panther Media GmbH/Alamy Stock Photo; 036: Marc Moritsch/National Geographic Creative/Alamy Stock Photo; 038: Power and Syred/Science Source; 042 BC: D. Kucharski & K. Kucharska/Shutterstock; 042 BR: Dragon Images/Shutterstock; 043: Aquapix/Shutterstock; 046: Inga Ivanova/Shutterstock; 045: BioPhoto Associates/Getty Images; 048: Eriklam/123RF; 050: Reuters/Alamy Stock Photo; 052 BL: Eye of Science/Science Source; 052 TR: Coneyl Jay/Getty Images; 053: Clive Gee/AP Images; 054: M. Watson/Ardea/AGE Fotostock; 062: Sheilaf2002/Fotolia; 063: Eurobanks/Fotolia;

Topic 2
066: Tonyz20/Shutterstock; 067: John Cancalosi/Alamy Stock Photo; 068: Blickwinkel/Alamy Stock Photo; 071 Bkgrd: Jo Crebbin/Shutterstock; 071 CR: Loop Images Ltd/Alamy Stock Photo; 072: Fototeca Gilardi/AKG Images; 074 T: Holmes Garden Photos/Alamy Stock Photo; 074 TCL: Russell Shively/Shutterstock; 076 BC: Westend61/Getty Images; 076 BR: Brian Kushner/Alamy Stock Photo; 080: Visual China Group/Getty Images; 082 TC: Pises Tungittipokai/Shutterstock; 082 TL: Nature Photographers Ltd/Alamy Stock Photo; 082 TR: Oli Scarff/AFP/Getty Images; 083: Nature Photographers Ltd/Alamy Stock Photo; 084: IrinaK/Shutterstock; 086: Kali9/Getty Images; 087 TC: Patricia Isaza; 087 TL: Zeljko

Radojko/Shutterstock; 088: IrinaK/Shutterstock; 089 BCR: All Canada Photos/Alamy Stock Photo; 089 TCR: REUTERS/Ulises Rodriguez/Alamy Stock Photo; 090: imageBROKER/Alamy Stock Photo; 094 TR: Angel DiBilio/Shutterstock; 095: Blickwinkel/Alamy Stock Photo; 096 BC: Sailorr/Shutterstock; 096 TC: Bazzano Photography/Alamy Stock Photo; 098: Martin Shields/Alamy Stock Photo; 099: Vodolaz/Fotolia; 100 BC: YAY Media AS/Alamy Stock Photo; 100 BR: Wwing/Getty Images; 101 BC: Scott Camazine/Alamy Stock Photo; 101 BL: The Science Picture Company/Alamy Stock Photo; 101 BR: Fabian von Poser/Getty Images; 102: Bildagentur Zoonar GmbH/Shutterstock; 104 BC: Steve Vidler/Alamy Stock Photo; 104 BR: Pedro Bernardo/Shutterstock; 107 CR: Barry Mansell/Nature Picture Library; 107 TR: Michelle Gilders/Alamy Stock Photo; 108: Saverio Gatto/Alamy Stock Photo; 110: Julia Clarke, Department of Geological Sciences, The University of Texas at Austin; 112: Vlad61/Shutterstock; 114: Vitstudio/Shutterstock; 117: Abeselom Zerit/Shutterstock; 118: Pallava Bagla/Getty Images; 121 B: Don Johnston/Getty Images; 121 CR: BGSmith/Shutterstock; 123: John Cancalosi/Science Source; 126 BL: Gallinago_media/Shutterstock; 126 BR: CLS Digital Arts/Shutterstock; 127: J Hindman/Shutterstock;

End Matter
130 BCL: Philippe Plailly & Elisabeth Daynes/Science Source; 130 BL: EHStockphoto/Shutterstock; 130 TCL: Cyndi Monaghan/Getty Images; 130 TL: Javier Larrea/AGE Fotostock; 131: Geoz/Alamy Stock Photo; 131: WaterFrame/Alamy Stock Photo; 132: Africa Studio/Shutterstock; 133: Jeff Rotman/Alamy Stock Photo; 134: Grant Faint/Getty Images; 135: Ross Armstrong/Alamy Stock Photo; 139: Martin Shields/Alamy Stock Photo; 140: Nicola Tree/Getty Images; 141: Regan Geeseman/NASA; 143: Pearson Education Ltd.; 144: Pearson Education Ltd.; 145 BR: Pearson Education Ltd.; 145 TR: Pearson Education Ltd.

Program graphics: ArtMari/Shutterstock; BeatWalk/Shutterstock; Irmun/Shutterstock; LHF Graphics/Shutterstock; Multigon/Shutterstock; Nikolaeva/Shutterstock; silm/Shutterstock; Undrey/Shutterstock

Take Notes

Take Notes

Use this space for recording notes and sketching out ideas.

Take Notes

Use this space for recording notes and sketching out ideas.

Take Notes

Use this space for recording notes and sketching out ideas.